THE UNFINISHED MYSTERY

john walchars

THE UNFINISHED MYSTERY

a crossroad book
THE SEABURY PRESS
NEW YORK

Second printing

1978
The Seabury Press
815 Second Avenue
New York, N.Y. 10017

Library of Congress Cataloging in Publication Data
Walchars, John.   The unfinished mystery.
"A Crossroad book."
1. Meditations. 2. Christian life—Catholic authors. I. Title.
BX2182.2.W33   242   77-16146   ISBN 0-8164-2184-6
Printed in the United States of America

Biblical quotations are from *The Jerusalem Bible*
Copyright © 1966, 1967 and 1968 by Darton, Longman & Todd Ltd
and Doubleday & Company, Inc.

The poetic epigraphs at the head of each chapter were
written by Virginia Malachowski.

I am grateful to Virginia Malachowski and Josephine Ryan for their perduring inspiration; to them I dedicate this book with joy.

CONTENTS

PREFACE

To see greatness decline creates greater pain than to watch smallness disappear, especially when the remaining ruins clearly show there once stood a proud castle. Historians can think easily in terms of civilizations coming and going, of empires rising and falling, of monarchies being overthrown and democracies established, but for those who live in the times of such turmoil it is hard indeed to accept the historical reality when one has loved what once was great.

The pointers on our clock are not yet stalled at midnight. Darkness does not cover our land. Evil is still recognized as evil and the good is praised as the thing to do. But the strength to be honest and faithful is waning. A flood of moral anarchy invades our boundaries and threatens values most dear to us. Those who still lead remarkable lives, who are true to their given promises, are as often scorned as imitated. As for our youth, although they are far more religious than their counterparts abroad, they are too confused, too uncommitted to stop the moral decline.

The founders of our country were convinced that the American experiment could not succeed unless it was

God-oriented. The spirit of faith prevailed in the simple homes of our ancestors, in the halls of our government, and in the intrepid heart of our growing nation. Never have we found it necessary to force God to leave our shores, to persecute his worshipers, or to declare his priests enemies of the state. Martyrdom was never an American experience.

Yet, though worship was free, God himself, the object of our worship, became more and more a stranger in our land. As a nation we have never hated God, but we haven't loved him too much either. To be hot or cold seems to make us uncomfortable, so we choose what he scorned, the lukewarm. Let saints be born in other countries.

We have been and still are a powerful nation. But if we ask power where it comes from, it must inevitably answer: Either from God or from man. There can be no other source. Whether shamed by its atrocities or thrilled by its beneficence, power either bows to heaven or adores the earth. And we, the living, face life's challenge and try to master it with either the blessing of the divine or with total reliance on the resources of this earth.

What inspirations are behind our performances in history? When all the curtains of secrecy and ignorance are lifted, what hands are holding our reins? Is power, in its dignity and integrity, replenishing morality in our hearts and on our earth, or is it siphoning off our faith and our virtues?

Perhaps it was our destiny to play more roles in modern history than any other nation. Especially when wars exhausted its crippled victims, the world looked to us for help. We never refused its pleas. We played our roles well, with no undue display of arrogance.

Today, the roles have changed. We grew old, although yet young, and when our voice is asked we are aware that we have become clumsy in shaping destiny through power. Could that be the reason why fewer and fewer nations seek our shield for their protection?

The idea of freedom as a right of all people everywhere is unique to our country. Asked from where this freedom comes, we must point to the creation of man whom God fashioned to his own likeness, free to roam and replenish the earth, free to decide what to do and where. Liberty was a flaming word, inspiring the vision that brought into being our new nation under God.

Hard as it is to explain the loss of freedom to those who take it for granted, it is even more difficult to awaken them to the dangers of a freedom that becomes license, where everyone does his own thing without any consideration for those affected by his actions.

Genuine freedom never implies absence of restraint. As long as it keeps within certain limitations which safeguard the rightful liberties of others, it is a hallowed blessing; but a selfish willfulness that scoffs at moral obligations to family, community, and the rest of the world becomes an ever more ruthless tyrant that destroys all freedom.

Freedom, always lost too late, can also be found too early. Maturity is necessary to relate to freedom honestly. To presume such maturity in early youth can be a serious mistake. If we could learn from past experiences, we would apply stricter discipline where it is most needed. But we live in an age which does not want to be reminded that, at times, greater love is needed to say No than Yes.

The roots of true freedom are found in faith, a faith

that inspires hope and love, and frees one from selfishness. A person whose inner self is free can hardly be corrupted, while one enslaved by his passions and greed is already corrupt. When inner freedom vanishes, a void is created, and who knows by what it will be filled? What fate can be more cruel than to be set free to encounter nothing but emptiness?

If suspicions and fears are corroding our society, isn't it because we are so eager to build a "free" society without a strong moral basis? Can we expect a harvest to ripen without first planting a seed? The seeds of change must first be planted and nurtured in our own hearts, for it is in the individual person that resurrection must be prepared.

May the reader of these chapters discover not only some of the mysteries hidden in his own life, but also discern some of the mysteries that anguish our nation. Old values forgotten or declared irrelevant rise before our minds and claim their right to be heard. "Stillness," jeopardized by our unceasing noise, invites us to pause and think. "Prayer" and "Meditation" lead us back to sources we gave up without realizing how much we were losing. "Weakness" and "Suffering" remind us of the frailty of our condition and our dependence on a higher being, while "Our Body" leads us to examine more carefully the role we assign to our physical forces in life. And "The Other" points out that all these thoughts lead us to the realization of the interdependency of all people with each other and the responsibilities we bear for those who share with us not only our country but, much more, the desires of our heart.

The land we live in is full of expectancy. What is

impossible today can become possible tomorrow. New avenues are asking to be opened, new tunnels to be dug, unchartered roads to be discovered. Complex problems, personal or global, call for daring solutions. If we fail in this mission we fail the expectations of humankind and at the same time undermine our creative partnership with God.

If we are too weak to hold the reins, others will step forward and take over. The one who will lead the way will always be the one who sees in the present moment the meaning of the coming one.

My hope is that *The Unfinished Mystery* will become a place to begin. If the reader feels encouraged, stronger perhaps than before, to bring forth life that is not yet born, then its message may turn on some lights that had been extinguished.

John Walchars, S.J.

THE UNFINISHED
MYSTERY

chapter 1

STILLNESS . . . . .

the desert

Today I searched the desert
Its wisdom to impart;
Instead I found a loveliness
Where stillness won my heart.

If you had a chance to stop the man on the street to question him about his dreams and desires, he would perhaps confess that all he wants is an escape to a faraway island where he can discover again what he has lost—inner stillness. Instead of saying, "Stop the world, I want to get off," he would simply stammer in near despair, "Stop the noise, I cannot bear it any longer."

Inner Stillness. What is it? Why do we need it so much? Isn't silence enough to cure the ills of modern civilization? Can't we just keep quiet and find this illusive peace which has become such a stranger to all of us?

It is in silence that we temper the power of our tongues to bring honesty and order into our speech, while in stillness we rule the emotions of our hearts to carry discipline and strength into our passions. Stillness covers a far wider region in the heart of man than silence since it drills much deeper into our souls.

Stillness, completely permeating the furrows of the heart, nourishes itself with the thought that God dwells in us and loves us as we are. The moment we surrender to this conviction without struggle or pain, the roots of stillness take hold and grow strong. If we refuse this knowledge, stillness will vanish from the sources of inner energies, leaving us empty and alone.

Stillness is not the pastime of the coward who is too timid to assert his mind or too frightened to claim the rightful share of his achievements. Nor can stillness ever be mistaken for the shyness of the lamb, which is an easy prey for the rapacious lion. Nor is it a flight into a Christianized Nirvana, in which we silence our needs and hunger to achieve tranquillity. Stillness, at its best, never flees from the harsh demand of our daily lives. It faces confidently all the burdens life enforces.

The man who searches for this precious gift of God will find in it a balance of powers which clearly indicates what he is able to do, while never forgetting what must be done. Its beneficial influence encourages an understanding of our own potential regarding the tasks at hand. It keeps our ever restless ambitions within the realm of wisdom, and it avoids extremes. "Yahweh, my heart has no lofty ambitions, my eyes do not look too high. I am not concerned with great affairs or marvels beyond my scope. Enough for me to keep my soul tranquil and quiet like a child in its mother's arms" (Ps 131:1-2).

Who needs stillness the most? Perhaps those who like it the least! Stillness provides the inner rest which is greatly needed by the man of action. Driven by a thirst for success, he instinctively converts his vitality into the outer dimensions of activity and motion. In order to attain earthly triumphs, he drives himself with no other thought in mind but more success and greater profits.

No one can abuse his inner riches without reaching levels of exhaustion, as no one can spend forever of his possessions without facing bankruptcy. The man of action, pressured by the strain of competition, is no exception to this law of the survival of the fittest. When resources vanish, leaving him fatigued and exhausted, when his rhythm of life is shattered and his balance broken, he must be alerted to the perils which can destroy him in his totality.

At this critical moment when danger signals flash around the switchboard of his life, the man of action must pause, cancel all his meetings, forget the tomorrow and return into his own desert to discover there again the foundations of serenity and peace. There will always be a place which is so different from the place he lives in where he can put aside all lessons learned and concentrate on the one demand of our Lord: "Peace! Be still!"

Stillness is also the welcomed guest of the man of speech. Convinced that he possesses a message worthy of sharing, the speaker listens not only to the voice of his own experience, great or small as it may be, but also to the voice of others who have achieved fame as speakers of their time.

Speaking carries the never-ending obligation of reading, learning, and exchanging ideas with those who have more experience and wisdom. Only by an impartial scrutiny of self will the speaker evaluate himself with honesty and avoid the curse of repetition. "Do not refrain from speech at an opportune time, and do not hide your wisdom; for wisdom shall be recognised in speech, and instruction by what the tongue utters. Do not contradict the truth, rather blush for your own ignorance" (Si 4:23–25).

Putting ideas into words drains not only the physical reservoir of strength but also taxes the mental stamina. Situations will inevitably arise when even the best of speakers become weary of delivery, question their affirmation and doubt their own convictions. Think of the many occasions experienced by all of us, where, in listening, we wished the speaker never had opened his lips. Isn't it a penance to endure an avalanche of words without meaning? How bored we feel to harken to a man without ideas to share. "Words from a wise man's mouth are pleasing, but a fool's lips procure his own ruin" (Qo 10:12).

A speaker, devoided of originality, has various options to choose from. He is free to leave the rostrum, which for some would be the best of all solutions; he can decide to continue delivering his speeches without challenging the expectations of his audience; or he can escape into stillness to search there for ideas which have never been found before. It might be long before the winter passes, but such a time of resurrection is necessary for the revival of the spirit. "Deep waters, such are the words of man: a swelling torrent, a fountain of life" (Pr 18:4).

There is another man left on our list for whom stillness must be the daily bread: the man of God. To kneel before the Almighty in front of the sanctuary and intercede for the needs of his flock can be a most moving experience for God's messenger on earth. The festival mood of Christmas, the solemnities of Easter, and the jubilations at Pentecost easily excite the imagination, and no one will file complaint against the drama of these blessed events. But to meet the face of God again and again, day in and day out, every hour of the day, presents a repetitious element which affects the man of God in a very different manner. There are some, too few perhaps, who flourish under the weight of their daily burdens, minding not at all the time spent in eternal praise of the divine. They are the saints amongst us sinners, making the world a better place to live in.

Temperaments, however, vary. What draws one closer to the love of God alienates another. To respond to the needs of the faithful, and to listen without hearing his own cries of hunger, can become too great a sacrifice for anyone whose heart is still divided by possessions. Human nature resents daily pressure, and in moments of fatigue the man of God is tempted to throw away the burdens of the Lord. A few take to flight while others, faithful to their promise, continue to fulfill their duties as shepherds of the Gospel watching over their sheep.

A price must often be paid. The service of the holiest turns into motions of routine and boredom. Meaningless words replace prayer, answers are given without thought, and gifts are dispensed without love. When this happens, the true man of God will move to reverse such a course of action. His own island of seclusion must be discovered in order to find the stillness that will reawaken his basic values of existence. "Go into your rooms, my people, shut your door behind you. Hide yourself a little while until the wrath has passed" (Is 26:20).

Action, speech, and service never walk away from stillness without first being enriched by its presence and saved by its power. Even today, as in days of old, the desert remains the secret fountain of hope and courage, inspiring those of us who see in life a mission which God and man together must fulfill.

Silence not born of stillness is counterfeit. Lips kept still simply to avoid contact with the other are not worthy of trust. To use this merely as a refuge, defensively fleeing the encounter, marks the gesture of a coward who cannot endure any confrontation. "There is the man who keeps quiet, not knowing how to answer, another keeps quiet, till the right moment, but a garrulous fool will always misjudge it" (Si 20:6–7).

Words often flow because we are at war with our own ideas. The more we are torn apart on the inside, the greater is the talk on the outside. When we are not able to live in peace with the beat of our own heart, we seek our security in an avalanche of sound, allowing talk to destroy the fiber of our mind. "The mouth of the fool works his own ruin, his lips are a snare for his own life" (Pr 18:7).

The real self seeks the security of stillness while the outer personality, the mask we wear, is loud and noisy. How often do conversations continue simply because we have nothing to say? And when such a contrived conversation exhausts itself, we feel empty and ashamed for having betrayed the precious gift of mind entrusted to us by our Lord for much better use.

To conclude, however, that speech is always on the witness stand in judgment of guilt or innocence would be primitive. Far from it, as speech can be the most effective means of communication given to us by God, who was the Word. It is only through speech that we are able to reveal to others who we are and who we are not. Every thought, imprisoned at first in the confines of the mind, bursts into freedom only through the wonder of speech. In speaking, not only can we take possession of a world, but we also can help to improve that world. Such a challenge is well worth the efforts of our most capable women and men.

Speech, like any other talent, is in constant danger of being abused. Possible abuse, however, should never deter the younger generation from studying speeches of the great men of our past to learn for themselves how to employ the magic of a word and master the structure of a powerful delivery. When speech camouflages the truth by turning a thought into a lie, it is not the fault of the speech but the intention of the speaker. "Lying is an ugly blot on a man, and ever on the lips of the ignorant. A thief is preferable to an inveterate liar, but both are heading for ruin" (Si 20:24–25).

Stillness possesses the enviable ability to interrupt the pointers of time and interject a pause in which new ideas are born and new worlds take beginnings. To formulate his dream, the great religious genius of the East, Buddha, readily exchanged the riches of his three palaces for the riches of stillness to find the wisdom he needed in solitude. John the Baptizer lived in the stillness of the desert until the day he appeared openly to Israel. Jesus of Nazareth, the most illustrious citizen to honor our world, was led by the spirit into the desert where he stayed for forty days without food. Holy Scripture tells us that when Jesus, who was God and Man, intended to pray to his heavenly Father, he fled into the stillness of the mountains in order to be alone to communicate with the peace of the heavens.

Great events in religious history are often accompanied by the magic of few words. The annunciation, the institution of the Eucharist and the death of our Lord on the cross are surrounded by very meager verbal accounts. In the Upanishads, one of the holy books of India, we read: "The sound of Brahman is OM. At the end of OM there is silence. It is a silence of joy. It is the end of the journey, where fear and sorrow are no more, steady, motionless, never falling, everlasting, immortal. It is called the omnipresent VISHNU. In order to reach the Highest, consider in adoration the sound and silence of Brahman, for it had been said: God is sound and silence. His name is OM. Attain therefore contemplation, contemplation is silence on HIM."* It seems that men without stillness never gather enough strength or courage to leap over their own shadow and come closer to their coveted ideal, the light of the sun.

Our brilliant twentieth century has made history with achievements of remarkable stature, deeds of greatness and wonder. At this very moment, our restless generation moves on with fascinating speed and astonishing determination in the fields of technology and science. No problem is too sacred to be left untouched, no human need too private to be exposed, and no subject too intimate to be scrutinized except for the questions—Where will all this movement lead us? and

---

* *The Upanishads*, translated and introduced by Juan Mascaró (Baltimore, Md.: Penguin Books, 1965), p. 102 (6:23).

Where will our progress end? At this very hour nearly every member of our nation is working to achieve a higher standard of living, without questioning for a moment what kind of an inspiration fans the fires of our triumphs. In the dramatic efforts to subdue and rule nature and inflame every corner of the universe with the torches of its Master, we brutally destroy eternal bonds to nature with an intensity never before perpetrated in the course of history.

Can anyone name the price which must be paid for the follies we have committed? In conquering the awesome stillness of the moon, have we become deaf to the desperate outcry of Mother Earth? Prophets have arisen to proclaim the imminent disasters and to denounce frivolities and sin, but has any civilization in its downfall ever reversed its course?

We must all reserve in our souls a place where all that is real can be accepted. The trivial, the cheap, and the noisy are the most advertised ideas in the markets today, and they are brought into our homes as the climax of perfection. Are not these strange failures, which some call chaotic, signs of a threatening disaster? Or is this chaos of ours only the beginning of a brighter tomorrow?

Contradictions have always torn man's soul apart; yet it is only when man takes his anxieties to verbal analysis instead of to inner stillness that these contradictions turn into problems. Stillness has never claimed a perfect record, nor does it pretend to solve all the riddles of man. The only promise stillness offers is to make the soul of man strong enough to rise above the threatening clouds of fear and live in harmony with the darkness. Those of us blessed enough to have experienced the healing effects of stillness have no doubt that it does exist.

Stillness farewell. Your dignity and charm have taken us by storm. Our eyes are open now to the mysteries and riddles which life in its complexities presents to us for solution. We perceive the meaning in all the lessons an ageless time has written to teach our noisy generation. Whether we are learning our lessons well, we do not know, but we are convinced, as we were never convinced before, that we need to learn what you alone can teach. In your proud land of stillness and serenity, our restless hearts find peace.

chapter 2

WEAKNESS . . . . .

the cloud

As clouds can mark a stormy sky,
My faults deny your name;
But fragile is the will, Oh Lord,
And weaknesses remain.

Whenever a situation arises which calls for us to describe ourselves, we are at once tempted to think in terms of strength: our intelligence, achievements, and special skills. To impress others, we characterize ourselves as trustworthy, of good taste, socially adept, intellectually perceptive, and especially as a person of vision. Somehow, when we list these impressive qualities, we do not feel that any injustice is done to our truthfulness or any harm is inflicted on those who have the privilege of sharing our company. God, when he called us to life, simply created a prelude to success, and for such an achievement, God must be praised!

In the same vein, when others are called upon to consider the finer points of our abilities, we expect them to compile a list of attributes so inclusive and far-reaching that it can only be received with envy and amazement. How soothing it is to our egos to learn that

11

we are thought of as incisive speakers, creative writers, efficient organizers,—even as being endowed with a jolly sense of humor! If anything is missing in us, it really cannot be very much. Were we to hang out a sign indicating our moral status, it would bear the simple message: Perfection. Any weakness, if existing at all, can only be understood as an embarrassing oversight in the otherwise flawless masterpiece of God's creation. Perhaps a secondary power in heaven's executive branch missed a point or two, and now we have to pay for this regrettable slip-up.

In our overall view of the human race, we look upon weakness as a disposable factor irrelevant to our blueprints or decision-making. Almost never do we think of it as an integral part of human nature. Like any other birth defect, we tend to hide it or totally deny it. Why call attention to something that shouldn't be there, or introduce a subject that only embarrasses ourselves and our listeners? The best we can do with it is to disregard its presence or camouflage it as virtue. There are some who can even declare it a sign of growing holiness! Who wants to appear less than perfect?

Considered purely as a natural human quality, weakness plays an ambiguous role in our life. Conscious of its lack of appeal, it creeps into hidden corners where it leads an unassuming but stubborn existence and refuses to be routed.

Whether inherited or acquired, weakness forms characteristics in all of us that are unique in structure and individual in expression. Like fingerprints, each is original, defying generalization. Being independent in its growth and influence, weakness does little to help us control its impact on us. Even an author who writes on weakness is often writing his own biography; one hardly needs to borrow insights from other people's lives when one's own experiences provide more than enough substance.

Individual weaknesses are cleverly concealed by those who are too frail to coexist with them. Vulnerable in their conceit, and easily hurt, they carefully avoid confrontation with anything that threatens their fantasy of perfection. And since applause is their chief goal in life, they sacrifice their real personality and allow a mask to take over.

A few who have reached the pinnacle of success are able to loose the tight rein of restraint and tell revealing tales of their weaknesses. They realize that greatness can appear more impressive when gained in spite of frailty and failures, and their confession of weakness therefore enhances rather than diminishes the brilliance of their halo. "For anyone who has will be given more, and he will have more than enough; but from anyone who has not, even what he has will be taken away" (Mt 13:12).

Unlike personal failings, weakness is inborn. It is an indestructable part of God's creation. No reason need be given for its existence, nor is care necessary for its growth. All it needs is a patient host.

But must we always think of God and his works only in terms of magnificence? Why cannot the weak and fragile also reflect his majesty? If it is his will that the less attractive things, born of weakness, have a rightful place in his creation to somehow signify his will, why should they not also appear at the center of events and assert their mission in the divine economy? The insignificant monotonies of life, cannot they also praise God's glory?

All of us are called to be God's faithful servants assisting the work of redemption. Whether in the roles of attractive saints and heroes or in the inconspicuous parts we play as workers in fields or factories, at desks or in coal mines, in hospitals or kitchens, we are all in the service of the honor and glory of God, transforming into worship all we do and all that we are. Whatever daily life contains, even the most insignificant deed, is worthy of being turned into prayer. "Whatever you eat, whatever you drink, whatever you do at all, do it for the glory of God" (I Co 10:31).

Weakness must not be confused with sinfulness. Sin and weakness are different in structure, motivation, and in their final effects. To compare the two is unjust. Sin destroys our intimate relationship with God, while weakness makes us more conscious of our need for his blessing. Sin exploits the autonomy of man; weakness stresses our dependence on the divine. Sin revolts, but weakness reaches out for peace.

Our inner health depends very much on our accepting weakness not as self-inflicted but as an integral part of our human nature. Unlike laziness, cowardice, maliciousness, which are personal deficiencies clamoring for correction, our weakness imposes on us the challenge to perform worthily despite our limitations. The coward cries, "I don't dare!" The one conscious of his weakness says, "I will do my best." "Another man is a poor creature begging for assistance, badly off for support, but rich in poverty, and the Lord turns a favorable eye on him, sets him on his feet out of his abject condition, and enables him to hold his head high, to the utter amazement of many"(Si 11:12–13). If we allow weakness to assume its proper role in life, even acknowledging it sometimes as a blessing in disguise, we are better off than those who live with self-deception. Weakness accepted and openly acknowledged might deflate the ego but it brings at the same time greater serenity that gives us a healthy balance. After all, most of us are adequate in many areas of life but handicapped in others, and if we set our goals within our reach and manage our resources wisely, we can lead a fruitful life in honesty and truth.

Looking at weakness only from a natural point of view is not giving it a full and just appraisal. It can also engender a certain spiritual energy that helps us in our self-evaluation. If we are conscious of our weakness as we analyze our problems, we see more clearly our dependence on God and humbly turn to him for guidance and sustenance. Thus, in the dialectic of the opposing forces in our lives, the spiritual assumes its rightful place.

When judging mankind, we find that the weakness of human nature exerts at least as strong an influence on historical decisions as any mark of perfection. Unless we understand the role it plays in worldly events, we do not understand history, and unless we understand its part in our own and others' fates, we do not understand the ways of God with man. Only weakness can explain many personal and historical events for which no other explanation can be found. And for that we must be grateful.

Whether weakness originates in the spirit or the body, it claims its rights and makes its powers felt in man's peculiar liability to suffer. Infirmity and anxiety are a part of our fate as much as the shadow is part of the sun. Who can be really sure of the arrival of tomorrow? Unexpected trials upset the plans of the most powerful people on earth. Cruel twists of fate, bringing death to body or mind, greet us when least expected. If we wait for a time or place where suffering no longer exists, then we wait for a dream never to be realized on this earth.

No one can silence our apprehensions about the powers of the unknown, and no one can assure us that everything will be all right. In all of our lives there remains the hill called Calvary, and the very moment we try to escape the cross we are stretched on its arms. "Happy indeed the man whom God corrects! Then do not refuse this lesson from Shaddai. For he who wounds is he who soothes the sore, and the hand that hurts is the hand that heals" (Jb 5:17–18).

Another aspect of human weakness is the incapacity to achieve in life all that one has planned. *There walks the person I wished to be* is heard more often than *Here walks the one I have created.* Few of us feel that we have actually achieved all that we hoped to do, and a sense of hostility toward the forces of nature sometimes rises in us because we feel cheated by the way life has handled our best intentions. Peevishly we count what life has given us and feel shortchanged. How often have we set out to find the gold at the end of the rainbow only to find ourselves stranded in a ditch? Frustrations overpower us, we feel let down, unable to get up again, not because we accept failure but simply because good luck has disappeared leaving us helpless in the mud.

If at times we are impatient about the course of our so-called normal life, when weakness blocks our highest aspirations and foils our most sincere desires, perhaps our cross would be lighter if we would remember that what happens to us is not due to the injustice or frivolity of fate but to our own share of weakness.

To be content with partial success is often better for our well-being than to expect the grand prize and be demoralized when it escapes our grasp. Christ himself, in his public life, had to live with many disappointments, not only from his own apostles but also from the leaders of his chosen people. Yet, bearing his weaknesses and failures, he fulfilled his mission and conquered the hearts of those he loved. "As the crowds were appalled on seeing him—so disfigured did he look that he seemed no longer human—so will the crowds be astonished at him, and kings stand speechless before him; for they shall see something never told and witness something never heard before" (Is 52: 14–15).

Human weakness is especially revealed in man's incapacity to protect himself. What means of defense is he endowed with when physically threatened or attacked? Of all the animals, the human one is the least prepared to defend himself. If assaulted, we can only scream and fend off danger with outstretched limbs. Helplessly, we close our eyes so as not to witness our own disaster. The woman raped, the old man beaten, the child abused, the victim tortured, all remind us in unmistakable terms how frail the human creature really is. To walk a road in darkness and be at the mercy of the brutal one who awaits us is not only an alarming sign of a deteriorating civilization but also a share of the weakness into which we were born and in which we must die. "Father, why hast thou forsaken me?"

Added to our physical inability to protect ourselves is another frustration. Our desire to preserve our body is hardly stronger than our determination to safeguard our economic stability. A financial collapse can destroy as much in a man as a physical collapse. Humiliating poverty can harm not only one's dignity but even one's spiritual potential. The old Irish saying, "Blessed be nothing," can be a wise warning. "Gold and silver will steady your feet; better valued than either, good advice. Money and strength make a confident heart; better than either, the fear of the Lord" (Si 40:25–26).

Of course it is wise to provide for the future, but to expect total economic and social security is presuming too much. Insecurity, as an integral part of the human condition, extends its reign, not only over our physical well-being but also over our economic status and our social environment. Permanent security on earth is as illusory as unmitigated bliss. All we can hope for if we carefully budget our resources without being overconcerned with money and possessions, is to acquire the inner freedom to enjoy life with both its poverty and its riches. "That is why I am telling you not to worry about your life and what you are to eat, nor about your body and how you are to clothe it. Surely life means more than food, and the body more than clothing! Look at the birds in the sky. They do not sow or reap or gather into barns; yet your heavenly Father feeds them. Are you not worth more than they are? Can any of you, for all his worrying, add one single cubit to his span of life? And why worry about clothing? Think of the flowers growing in the fields; they never have to work or spin; yet I assure you that not even Solomon in all his regalia was robed like one of these. Now if that is how God clothes the grass in the field which is there today and thrown into the furnace tomorrow, will he not much more look after you, you men of little faith?" (Mt 6:25–30).

Other faces, too, are hidden in the realm of weakness. Take, for instance, shame and our difficulty in warding it off. Shabby deeds and careless thoughts lead us often enough into situations that are less than honorable. Against our better judgment we pursue a course which leads to a sorry conclusion. We load our conscience with burdens which we must bear alone in shame. When Adam, disturbed by God's indictment, tried to blame poor Eve for his predicament in paradise, Eve in her embarrassment quickly turned and condemned the serpent for the disgrace she had to suffer. However, when God assessed the final situation, he expelled both of them from the blissful garden, apparently convinced that the guilt was equally divided. "Because you listened to the voice of your wife and ate from the tree of which I had forbidden you to eat, accursed be the soil because of you" (Gn 3:17).

Burdens of shame are not easy to bear. The effect of a wrongdoing is unpleasant enough to live with, but to endure the inner torment caused by our transgressions calls for uncommon strength. No wonder, then, that quite a few of us are eager to blame someone else for what we have brought about ourselves. How easy it is to point the finger outward rather than inward, to cry: "Your fault!" instead of "Mea culpa!"

As part of our weakness, shame is often linked to failures experienced in the greatest human adventure—love. Romantic love, the happy festival of life, can unfortunately also generate its invidious counterforces of exploitation, seduction, jealousy, and the desire to domineer. Is anything more difficult in life than to love in total honesty or to discern with certainty what is genuine love and what is its counterfeit? Exercising the shameful technique of the egotist who seeks only his own satisfaction is to indulge in the allurements of love while escaping its responsibilities. But have we not all felt shame in our hearts when we declared our love for another and found that, unconsciously, self-love was our motive? To respond with passion when love is asked is to betray the hope of the beloved, and for such a betrayal shame will be the price.

If love is the great magnifier, shame is the sure diminisher. Emotions excited by love double our energies, while feelings of shame paralyze us. Love seeks knowledge and revelation, shame wants only to hide. In love we outdo ourselves in delightful ways; in shame we are bereft of all delight. "Let us lie down in our shame, let our dishonour be our covering, for we have sinned against Yahweh our God" (Jr 3:25).

Each sentiment in our world of emotions claims its corresponding object. Greed relates to possessions, jealousy to love, pride to the intellect. Shame overrides them all, asserting its power over all our affections, passions, and sensitivities. It plays its part in our laziness, our stubbornness, and all the less flattering facets of our personality. Only the person shamed can tell what blushes in his mind and disturbs his heart, and he alone can remove its cause. Not always, however, are our humiliations caused by our own follies. Occasions arise when frivolous friends or malicious enemies do harm to our reputations and to our peace of mind. And yet, to seek revenge in such a predicament can be as demeaning as to clamor too loudly for justice. A better remedy is to remember our own weaknesses and the many undiscovered blunders we have made. If we insist on remaining always blameless and are never subjected to injustice, we take away from life the tension that builds up a mature character. Besides, should we expect perfection in others when we cannot discover it first in ourselves?

In spite of all its embarrassing qualities, shame fulfills a function in the gradual maturation of our personality. In the deeper recesses of our being, it fosters the will to be decent in our actions and modest in our thoughts. A generation without shame is hardly worth the effort it takes to save it. Moral values are the backbone of our culture, and to tamper with them is to undermine the very security upon which our whole society and the humaneness of all mankind rests. We can already see the portents of the recent flood of immorality and corruption in our society. To hope that the moral fiber of our people will not be seriously impaired by it is an expectation that history cannot grant. "My son, bide your time and be on your guard against evil, and have no cause to be ashamed of yourself; for there is a shame that leads to sin, as well as a shame that is honourable and gracious"(Si 4:20–21).

Saint Paul seems to have assumed the role of articulate spokesman for all of us when he freely confessed the weakness which manifests itself in contradictions and confuses our behavior. Haven't we all experienced these contradictions when we have tried to coordinate our desires with our actions, to put our ideas into deeds? The good we see we often neglect to perform, and the evil we detest somehow we do.

So many times we have at our disposal the means to execute a mission of love, yet our actual performance steers in the opposite direction. Though we really want to share with others, and have enough earthly treasures at our disposal, when the moment of decision arrives, we put the money into our own account. Can anyone explain what really happens when, in certain situations, we are eager to act unselfishly but turn in a selfish and ungracious performance instead? What kind of powers are at work in us when our noblest intentions result in something ignoble? What a short step it is from saint to sinner! And what a small inch divides the hero from the knave! "I cannot understand my own behaviour. I fail to carry out the things I want to do, and I find myself doing the very things I hate"(Rm 7:15).

Mankind, after all, is not perfect. Perhaps God could have tried a little harder and come up with a being who had no flaws, but he did not. If there is anyone who is never tempted, never irritated or frustrated, he must live on another planet. Ruler over many forces, man is ruled by other forces which he cannot tame. We marvel at the wonders his genius has created, yet we are appalled by the squalor he must endure in order to survive. He is at once the master who dominates and the helpless being who is dominated.

But let us not become disheartened. Weakness is not expressed only in disabilities, incapacities, and other negations; it has also positive functions to fulfill.

Recognized and acknowledged, weakness reveals to us what we are, what we can do, and what is beyond our strength. In this role it can be an appreciated friend. Those who think they can plunge headlong into life and freely shape their destinies to their extravagant blueprints will gain wisdom and maturity only when they accord to weakness its proper share in their decision-making.

Even more important is the strength and depth which the knowledge of our weakness gives to our human relationships. Only through our own experience can we begin to relate profoundly to others in their weaknesses. How much sympathy or empathy has one who has never suffered? Can we ever fully apprehend the quandary of the derelict if we have never felt deprived ourselves? Not until we ourselves have journeyed through the tunnel of darkness can we say to the other, "Now I know what hell you have endured." Only when we have experienced sorrow and defeat in our own souls can the message of Christ, so consoling to the afflicted, move our hearts and motivate our actions when we meet our suffering brothers and sisters.

Paul's declaration, "When I am weak I am strong" can refer not only to the human condition but also to the Church in which we Christians experience our humanity. Somewhere in the world the Church is always suffering, somewhere in the world it is nailed to a cross. Looking back on its history we cannot fail to note the ruins of the best of its dreams as well as the effects of its most splendid achievements. For the Church, as for many other institutions, history has been kind and cruel at the same time in different parts of the globe.

Today, as in other ages, the Church is suffering. Defections tear at its soul in large numbers while some of its most faithful disciples endure cruel persecutions. Altercations surround its altars, and fewer and fewer accept its voice as perfect and as final. Traditional expressions which were the Church's unifying power for centuries are abandoned at a time when clear and timely redefinitions of the unchanging values would have comforted a bewildered and confused flock. Things held sacred for many generations are held irrelevant at the very time when men's troubled minds need to turn to the truly sacred for hope. Interpretations sustained by outdated sources prove inadequate to cope with the discoveries of a new creative technological epoch; and modern man, sensing his opportunity, conceives new symbols to fill the void.

No one can say that the Church has abandoned its treasures of divine revelation or that it has sacrificed truths and principles for the sake of convenience. Rather, what disturbed the needle of the compass and steered the flock into alien paths was the timing, the phrasing, and the authoritarian presentation of unpopular positions unrelated to revelation.

It is not suggested that the Church should formulate its dogmas and teachings according to the whim of its constituents—only political parties can afford such a dubious luxury—but greater sympathy and respect for the moral and social dilemma of the ordinary sinner would have been a more Christlike and successful course. We realize that the voice of the people is not always the voice of God, but the conscientious judgment of a faithful people may often mirror more of the divine plan than the learned pronouncements of churchmen who live alone in reasonable comfort.

Wisdom and understanding are needed when we are confronted with the anxiety and problems of our loyal followers. To grant them the freedom they need to express their thoughts, and not to smother their voice before it is really heard, is the duty of the shepherd who loves his flock. To make decisions after listening to what they can teach us is a wiser course than to repeat the answers in the book.

But even an awareness of lost possibilities is a significant sign of growth. As long as the Church appears only as a stern-talking organization managed from a safe distance, it will never be able to live up to the demands of its divine mission. Today's Church must become again a center and inspiration for a renewed civilization if civilization as we know it is to survive. If it fails to proclaim by example as well as by words the standards proclaimed by Christ, other standards will move in and absorb the souls of our people—an exchange that will not be for the better. "He who is not with me is against me, and he who does not gather with me scatters" (Mt 12:30).

To see shadows falling on the very sanctuary where the Holy of Holies rests can burden timid souls. But perhaps we should remember that it is often our own weakness that reflects in the troubled face of the

Church. A stubborn nostalgia for bygone glories, a sentimental attachment to exterior manifestations of our belief, can delay a necessary process which must be undergone in order to compete with the tremendous forces of our explosive century. A past that cannot become a part of our present should be forgotten.

Faith and faith alone can overcome the obstacles we find in the Church. If our eyes are scandalized by what they see, if our ears are smarting from what they have to listen to, if our sensitivities are hurt by what they must endure, let us take refuge in our beginnings, our apostolic heritage, and find there again the Truth and the Way, free of the burdens which the centuries have accumulated.

The Church is not dying, but something *in* the Church has to die to give way to the stirrings of a new and better life. We are called upon by history, not by choice, to witness the transition from values cherished in the past to values of a future which has not yet arrived. To be faithful to our Church in transition, as the first Christians were to a Church in persecution, is our special task today. "For if anyone is ashamed of me and of my words, of him the Son of Man will be ashamed when he comes in his own glory and in the glory of the Father and the holy angels" (Lk 9:26).

Whenever we attach conditions to our affections, we ask a price no honest love will pay. To follow our Church in spite of its failures and contradictions, to accept it with all its weakness is the way of a love that will endure the test of time.

chapter 3

SUFFERING . . . . .

the rain

In suffering, I share your love,
And yet the tears remain;
But soon will come my time of
*   peace*
As sunshine follows rain.

Man has been described as a creature composed of body and soul. Both elements require careful attention. The soul, the invisible partner, unexpectedly fascinates man more than the demands of the visible body, which he takes for granted. The body is fed, driven, enjoyed, and abused, and many times is forgotten until the mechanism of this magnificent machine stalls. At that moment man falls apart. He was not prepared for pain.

Where is the person who freely chooses suffering? If we could determine our seasons, how many would want the winter's chill? Who would lean toward a center of grief if an escape route to joy were open? Just as the apostles fled the torment of defeat, so would we flee the darkness if we had the choice. Contentment, after all, attracts our imagination far more than calamity. Very few would be strong enough to ask that the cross "be mine as I am yours." St. Paul assured the Corinthians that "You can trust God not to let you be tried beyond your strength, and with any trial he will give you a way out of it and the strength to bear it" (I Co 10:13).

As dry soil yearns for the relief of showers, our arid souls yearn for the strength which anguish provides. One who has never faced the threat of failure can easily remain immature, embracing life more in frivolity than in challenge. In the bliss of our ignorance, we offer childish insights which delude those who need the values of experience and wisdom. The obvious is the only ground on which immaturity can function.

If we ourselves are never tested, how can we understand the tests of others? If we are never cut by the sword of pain, how can we respond to another's agony? Who can unravel all the mysteries of life without having been probed by grief? We grow stronger within by the sufferings imposed upon us from outside forces. It is the healthy branches that withstand the tempest and grow continually through the ordeal, while the lifeless ones break under the onslaught and rot away.

Storms and upheavals never fashion the features of man; they only reveal what kind of person he was before the violence tore at his roots. The pressures of grief expose us to a knowledge no other power can reveal. It is then that we know our strengths and our weaknesses and our real self takes a bow!

The delicate question, "Who am I?" is never so candidly answered as in the moment a demanding Lord fills our heart with sorrow. It is not too presumptuous to say, "Tell me how you suffer and I can tell you who you are."

Sorrow and grief can wreck one's harmony of mind, but many of us would never reach maturity without the lessons they teach. People often lose their God when he speaks to them through pain and tribulation, while the same trials will bring others to a better understanding of how God views our existence.

Heaven is never so partial that it selects its citizens from the ranks of sufferers only. Other roads lead to the pinnacle of sanctity. Intense work for God's eternal glory and the fearless preaching of the joyous tidings also secure a favorable reception at the gate of paradise. A variety of personalities and characters which make life on earth so interesting will also be found in the world which is yet to come. "God has put them to the test and proved them worthy to be with him; he has tested them like gold in a furnace, and accepted them as a holocaust" (Ws 3:5–6).

Even philosophers who reject faith as a reality admit that pain makes an important contribution to the betterment of the human character. Failures, which are hurdles man must learn to take, are more challenging than pure logic or mathematical abstractions. Dialectic laws, supposed to work with infallible accuracy, turn into a living process in which suffering and death make the final decision. The art of learning to withstand pain checks the flight into inertia. Adversity always influences reality.

In science, progress is achieved to the degree that we overcome the obstacle; yet failures can stimulate values which otherwise would never come to light. Great discoveries were made in times of war and other natural disasters. Scientists study their theories more carefully when they are contradicted; writers choose words more thoughtfully if critics lie in wait. Historical facts that are seemingly unchangeable can also take on a new light when they are challenged by disagreement. All of us can admit that we have learned more from people who were critical of our actions than from those who showered us with praise. Undoubtedly in all of us there is a particular part of the ego which flourishes best the moment it is resisted. Surely we can hardly hope to learn much from those who know only how to applaud.

What is true for the world of science is also true for the world of faith, where science is not contradicted but is excelled. What challenges the minds of our great thinkers has challenged much more the hearts of our saints. "Happy indeed the man whom God corrects!" (Jb 5:17).

God chose suffering as the center of redemption. Death and life became so intertwined in the life of our savior that one cannot abide without the other. It was in death that life was born and in suffering that resurrection dawned. The cross was needed to realize forgiveness; the gloom of calvary had to precede the glories of Easter.

Christ did not welcome the torture inflicted on his perfect body by the nails and thorns. He did not like the idea of hanging on a cross while the Romans gambled away his meager garments. There was no intimation that his final hours of agony brought delight to his emaciated body. All he expressed was the wish not to suffer, the desire to avoid the chalice prepared for him by his heavenly Father. "Yet he was pierced through for our faults, crushed for our sins" (Is 53:5).

Redemption could have taken place without the

elements of painful suffering. A decision of the divine
will would have sufficed to pay the debts we have
incurred. Through Christ, a heavenly decree could
have been promulgated announcing that all sins were
forgiven by the triumvirate in heaven and Calvary
would never have appeared on our map of redemption. But that was not what God had in mind. "You
foolish men! So slow to believe the full message of the
prophets! Was it not ordained that the Christ should
suffer and so enter into his glory?" (Lk 24:25-26).

Christ had to suffer, not only because he wished to
honor the prophecies and insure redemption but because his beloved Father freely proposed it to him.
And he, the obedient son, made the Father's wish his
law. "It was essential that he should in this way become completely like his brothers so that he could be a
compassionate and trustworthy high priest of God's
religion" (Heb 2:17).

Mencius, one of the old Chinese sages, showed pro-
found discernment for the value of suffering when he
said: "Whenever heaven wants to confer a great work
on anyone, it first drenches his heart with bitterness,
submits his nerves and his bones to weariness, deliv-
ers his members and his whole body to hunger, reduces him to the most extreme indigence, thwarts and
upsets all of his enterprises. By this means, it awakens
in him good sentiments, fortifies his patience, and
communicates what was still lacking in him." After
illustrating this principle with historical events, Mencius concluded: "From these things we see how life
springs from sorrow and tribulations, while death re-
sults from ease and pleasure."

Gautama Buddha, the enlightened one, preached

that pain and afflictions are inherent in the very life process, which is characterized by change and impermanency. Nothing in life is constant, everything is subject to mutation. Our thoughts, hardly born, turn into other thoughts, and new experiences replace the older ones which have scarcely had time to ripen. That there will be change is the one unchanging law of life.

The nature of our existence can never be fully understood. We yearn for lasting security in an insecure world. To hunger without ever finding total satisfaction is our fate. In our craving for the riches which the world cannot provide, we bring forth our own sufferings. Only when our journey on earth comes to an end will this craving cease and the suffering vanish.

To submit to the reality of suffering without losing hope is the truth of suffering. Why the greatest men in history took suffering into their hearts and let it become the center of their teaching will never be fully understood. The why of suffering remains for God alone to clarify when we see him face to face. Yet with this mystery, God gives strength to bear the sorrow as it is sent. No one will ever be tested beyond endurance. Unlike sensual joys, which lose appeal upon reaching the height of fulfillment, suffering becomes so intense that we believe we cannot bear any more; but when more comes, we *are* able to face it. "The trials that you have had to bear are no more than people normally have" (I Co 10:13).

To live with a mystery requires faith, and the strongest kind of faith is necessary if we are to accept affliction as a message from heaven. God takes us on as worthy partners in his gigantic task to free the world from its own chains. He appointed us as partakers of the mystery to make up what is still missing in the sufferings of Christ. If it is true that God is our hope in heaven, it is equally true that we are God's hope on earth. Like Job, we must be as strong in pain as we are in joy, for after all, "If we take happiness from God's hand, must we not take sorrow too?" (Jb 2:10).

If it is our duty to help in the task of creation, it is also our obligation to accept our share of the cross as a part of our redemption. Were anyone free of guilt, he could protest the assignment, but with our recognition of sin, we all must bow to the divine decision. Heaven, in all of its glory, will reveal the secrets we do not now comprehend. God must be seen in his great kindness so that the burdens will be lightened and our faith confirmed. "This is a cause of great joy for you, even though you may for a short time have to bear being plagued by all sorts of trials; so that, when Jesus Christ is revealed, your faith will have been tested and proved like gold" (I P 1:6–7).

Questions and doubts often arise which strain our intimate relationship with God. Our vision is usually so narrow it cannot fully grasp the depth of God's redemption, while our hunger for pleasure is so intense it resents infringement from beyond. No matter how strongly we wish to believe in God's divine compassion, unresolved tensions easily mar the acceptance of divine decision when there is a cross to bear.

Why not a world in which tranquillity and peace prevail? Why do we threaten, hurt, and kill each other in order to safeguard our own survival? Why must we continue senseless wars which only solve the problem of overpopulation by killing reluctant soldiers and innocent witnesses? How can we hear the message of

God's love when deadly cells advance on avenues which crisscross our body? Shouldn't all evil be eradicated from the earth so that the good can finally triumph?

Faith would not be faith if it answered all of our questions and provided solutions to all of our riddles. Incomprehensibility is only one of the attributes that graces the nature of the divine. To believe, especially in moments when we can not see clearly, and to submit wholeheartedly when everything revolts against submission, is the herioc surrender asked of all who hope to enter heaven.

To doubt that there is a higher intelligence—dare we call it a higher sense of humor—in charge of humanity is to credit human reason with a supremacy completely beyond its reach. All of our experiences with the human mind, as startling as they might be in moments of great achievement, make it painfully clear to all of us that the wonder of creation demands explanations no earthly power can ever provide. "Lord who shall we go to? You have the message of eternal life, and we believe; we know that you are the Holy One of God" (Jn 6:68–69).

Organic diseases are not the only test with which we have to reckon; psychological illness must also be added to the list of woes. The mind can summon feelings which are so close to pain that pain itself is mystified by its beginning and end. We grow tense with anxiety, our muscles tighten, breathing is stifled, and the heartbeat quickens until the body reacts with psychogenic pains. We ache as much from this as from any visible wound in our body.

Very often, in serious minded patients, hallucinations occur stimulating sensations, so-called phantom pains, truly experienced by patients who have lost a limb in an accident or operation. Guilt feelings can exert such pressures they distort our rationality and upset the rhythm of the inner clock that signals health or pain. The question "Am I right or wrong?" involves the mind as well as the body.

Who knows which sufferings are more distasteful, the outer ones harassing our bodies or the inner ones disfiguring our souls? Do we hurt more when our flesh suffers or when our mind smarts? Where are we the more vulnerable? Is being unwanted a greater hardship than actual physical pain? Is a lack of love a more deeply felt privation than the lack of one of our senses? "But I will make the blind walk along the road and lead them along paths. I will turn darkness into light before them and rocky places into level tracks" (Is 42:16).

It is almost impossible to transmit the experience of suffering into the hearts of those who have never lived it. Can a cross be fully understood before we have borne its weight? Darkness cannot be borrowed, it has to be endured.

History is, after all, a very poor teacher. Only rarely does humanity accept a lesson from the anguish and distress of others. It is easier to transplant organs into our bodies than danger signals into our hearts. We all prefer the anticipation of joy over the preparation for pain.

What is it that prevents us from being open to the warnings? Is our own insecurity so preeminent that we refuse the added burdens which might upset our delicate balance? Are political or moral dangers a thorn in our side because they threaten our comfortable living? Are prophets who predict a chaos doomed because they announce a truth which is not pleasant to hear?

To wear a blindfold in order to avoid the naked truth of life creates a world which is as defenseless as any world of the past. "You have made the earth tremble, torn it apart; now mend the rifts, it is tottering still! You have allowed your people to suffer, to drink a wine that makes us reel" (Ps 60:2–3).

Spiritual life progresses only to the degree that we raise ourselves from the level we have already reached to the higher one which beckons. A period of stagnation, dressed in leisure and relaxation, is often plagued by symptoms of sterility and boredom. When self-complacency refuses to learn from the lessons that tomorrows can teach, the tomorrows will arrive without hope and without meaning. When our soul is wounded by the strain of affliction, we must decide whether to allow the wound to heal or simply to close. Remaining vulnerable to more suffering, whether it arrives or not, is a good way to learn from sorrow.

Those who think they have experienced the full lesson of suffering are to be pitied more than envied. Their horizons narrow to the point where they seem to exist without a sense of failure, completely unaware that it is the failure itself which has gradually become the whole of their life-style. Books can be laid aside when read, but life's story with its infinite mystery defies an end to learning. And such learning is never more needed than in the moment of crisis. It is then that we are probed under the scrutiny of God and man, and there are no hiding places.

With faith and trust as our only armor, we have to step forward into the complexities of life and realize that God is alive as a tremendous force to be reckoned with. "My grace is enough for you: my power is at its best in weakness. So I shall be very happy to make my weaknesses my special boast so that the power of Christ may stay over me" (II Co 12:9–10).

Suffering is never imposed for the sake of suffering alone. The cross of Calvary was not holy because it was a cross; it was holy only because Christ carried it on his shoulders. Christianity teaches us that suffering is one of the best means of spiritual growth, leading our minds and our hearts to the sources where ultimate values can be discovered.

The saints disliked their pains as much as we do but they loved Christ so much they accepted their share of bitterness and failures as an integral part of their redemption. To find an answer where others only find more questions is one of the greatest blessings faith provides.

Almost all suffering is bearable if we are assured of a time when the onslaught of afflictions will lose its grip on our life. The promise of an end in sight awakens the moral courage we need to get a firm hold on our spiritual resources which can transform the crisis into a challenge.

Sufferings which increase without end can be fatal to the spirit of man. Not to know when it will be over, not to hear the news that relief is near, not to see the glimmer of hope on the desolate horizon, is a knowledge which tears into the flesh of man as cruelly as any suffering on earth.

The vitality of the will to resist has been broken in

some of our greatest people the moment they heard the news that everything was lost. The realization that no power in the world can reverse their fate, that no one can heal their wounds, drains away the last source of survival, the will to conquer. In the truest sense, it can then be said that everything is lost.

Yet this agony which seems to contain few redeeming features can also hold the promises of the greatest hope we can ever entertain. Losing all on earth can mean, sometimes, gaining everything for heaven. The final destiny of life, which lies in the fulfillment of happiness in the world to come, is the nearest to our reach the very moment earthly securities collapse.

So much depends on our inner motivations, on the way we submit to the mystery of our suffering. While one walks right into the sadness of his own funeral, the other steps triumphantly into the glory of his own resurrection. Where we find ourselves will depend on decisions each of us makes alone.

chapter 4

PRAYER . . . . .

the mountain

All that the world can ever be
Shall be, Oh Lord, because of thee;
A work of joy which I can see,
A mountain formed with love for
me.

If it is hard to capture the magnificence of a sunrise, how much more difficult to capture the power of prayer. Both of these experiences are of such splendor it is a challenge to describe their greatness. One lights up a sleepy earth; the other awakens an expectant heaven. The sunrise begins each day anew while the power of prayer continues without end.

PRAYER IS FAITH ALIVE

Spiritual energies, born of a strong conviction, penetrate the whole of our being. Questions and answers assume different proportions and find solutions which purely natural reasoning could never furnish. God is felt more in realization than in expectation. Belief not only arouses a mental curiosity that stimulates the intellect, but it generates a living force to sustain us in our periods of need. Faith alive becomes the central point where questions are resolved in a light of divine origin. Through its power, moral values surface and reflect our true worth. If we identify clearly with the demands of such a faith, a certain feeling of security gradually replaces the threats of the unknown. How can fear paralyze the willpower of anyone able to gain strength through the power of prayer? "Stay awake, praying at all times for the strength to survive all that is going to happen, and to stand with confidence before the Son of Man" (Lk 21:36).

PRAYER IS FAITH EXPRESSED

According to our need or our mood, we might shout to God in jubilation or revere him in deep silence. At times we sing to God with joyful voices while at another time we prefer a book to read prayers used before.

Since God is receptive to either the spoken or unspoken word, greater importance should not be given to meditation than to simple oral prayer. The motives which inspire our supplications are of more importance than our manner of expression. When the apostles asked Christ to teach them to pray, Christ answered, "Say this when you pray: Father, may your name be held holy, your kingdom come; give us each day our daily bread, and forgive us our sins, for we ourselves forgive each one who is in debt to us. And do not put us to the test" (Lk 11:2–4).

In prayer we say "I believe" with a voice as strong as our faith. If we base our acceptance of God on personal experience, prayers will be genuine. If, however, faith is used only to offset fears or honor customs, prayers can be as lifeless as the lips that murmur the words. "Hypocrites! It was you Isaiah meant when he so rightly prophesied: This people honours me only with lip-service, while their hearts are far from me. The worship they offer me is worthless; the doctrines they teach are only human regulations" (Mt 15:7–9).

The moment we give up our faith, we give up our prayer. One cannot exist without the other. If we consider belief in divine intervention to be only a sign of outmoded piety, what else is left for us to fall back on but our own cunning? Isn't this inviting failure?

Faith lost and faith not yet discovered are of different dimensions. The man who is still searching for God has not yet unveiled the mystery of prayer, while the one who has given up God has already lost it. The atheist might be better off than the believer who gambles away his spiritual heritage, because the atheist is not yet born, while the one who has sacrificed his belief is no longer alive.

PRAYER IS FAITH LISTENED TO

In a discourse between God and man, God speaks the first sentence, he takes the initiative. Man might be first in the animal kingdom, but in the divine kingdom he comes second. Before we can be speakers, we must learn to be listeners.

In prayers, we encounter Christ. He is heard in our Scripture, worshiped in our liturgy, and sought as refuge in our trials. We have to discover him first in our own prayers in order to hear his voice in the petitions of others.

Christ is the light in which we recognize truth, the way that orients our destiny. Our lives are shaped through the powers set free by the mystery of incarnation. By listening to his words, we receive the wisdom to open up new roads into life. "Send out your light and your truth, let these be my guide, to lead me to your holy mountain and to the place where you live" (Ps 43:3).

Before we find God in our prayer, we must find each other in our love. God himself warns us not to approach him unless we are at peace with others. Forgiving love warms not only our own heart but unites all of us standing in the presence of the divine. To pray for the needs of another and to forget our own is to reach toward the heights where God's gifts and our poverty find a blessed meeting place. In man, we meet God.

A prayer for another does not necessarily call for words or ceremonies; it can be the patient listening to tales of sorrow, or the simple compassion with the pain of the other. It is found in the long vigil of protection for the one we love, or a sharing of darkness with a neighbor. Whatever form our petitions assume, they must be real enough to touch the heart of God.

Sensitivity for the needs of those around us and sensitivity for the demands of God are so intimately linked with each other that one depends on the other for complete fulfillment. More than ever is the holiness of God confronted with the frailty of man. To pray to a God "outside there" to avoid the ills of man "inside here" is using prayer as an escape rather than an act of worship. The more willing we are to alleviate the pressures which others endure, the more willing the others will be to believe.

If prayers open our lips without touching our hearts, they are meaningless to those who seek the love of God in our love for them. "Anyone who says 'I love God', and hates his brother, is a liar, since a man who does not love the brother that he can see cannot love God, whom he has never seen" (I Jn 4:20).

Prayer is a risk. The voice that is expected to answer our petitions is physically absent. We believe in God's spiritual reality, but we realize it remains forever an invisible mystery. How often do we flounder in the darkness, frightened by the thought that God is unreachable? He calls us to walk by his side but he never appears. To cry out in loneliness and find ourselves even more alone does little to lighten our burden. Loneliness seeks company and if God is too far away, other emotional needs might overshadow our spiritual yearnings. The one who can bring us to God can also separate us from him.

Prayer has more disguises than actors have roles. Despair or exultation seeks its cover and superstitions claim it for protection. It is a refuge for lost courage yet gives strength to bear a cross. Remembered when rain is wanted, it is forgotten when the weather suits our need.

For the atheist, speaking to God is typical of a telephone conversation with no one at the other end; and to invite people to dialogue with a supreme being is a cruel hoax since all they really get is a useless monologue with themselves. The sooner prayer is outlawed, they contend, the better for all concerned.

What the atheist denies, the agnostic doubts. Not really sure about anything in his religious outlook, the agnostic questions both the existence of God and his nonexistence. Why pray if we are not sure that anyone is listening, he asks?

For the innocent, prayer is a marvel. They pray for snow and find that snow is falling; they pray for sunshine and watch the clouds disappear. Is there anything in the world that their prayers cannot accomplish?

The aged seek consolation in prayer, when all other consolations fail. With life coming rapidly to its end, they are eager to secure some stronghold in the world to come and feel nothing can do that better than prayer.

The sphere of influence of prayer includes those who have left us for a better world. A prayer for the deceased is our last embrace for the one dear to our memory. Since we cannot do anything for their lifeless body, we can beg God's mercy for their eternal souls. "For if he had not expected the fallen to rise again it would have been superfluous and foolish to pray for the dead" (II M 12:44).

Some say that prayer is as natural as breathing, but this has to be accepted with some reservation. In every civilization past, inscriptions or paintings were found which clearly recorded belief in the existence of deities whose magic powers were interwoven with the cultural development. There was always an altar surrounded by a revered priesthood set apart to intercede with the different gods for the needs of the people. Even in the most primitive beginning of humanity, there was the worship of gods and goddesses whose duty it was to protect the good and drive away the evil. Archaeologists, perhaps more than theologians, can attest to the fact that prayer has ever been a universal hunger.

But what is summarized from the many is not always shared by the one. What comes naturally to our race is not always natural to the individual. Some never seem to sense the need to beg from God a gracious blessing, while others pray only when dangers encroach upon their comfort. Have we not all, at times, put God aside until a ceremony calls for his presence?

Independence is one of the better human qualities. Adolescents leave their homes to prove they can make the journey alone. Security is thrown away and new beginnings appear on their map of the future. God, too, becomes a victim of the stormiest period in life when youth declares himself "omnipotent." Let God be busy with his heavenly kingdom, says the young, I will settle my own affairs on earth. God is not declared an enemy but a relic of the past and no longer useful.

Total reliance on self tempts not only the younger generation but whets the appetite of the mature as well. Should success greet us at every corner, we are apt to become self-sufficient to such a degree that we offer to God only the slightest attention.

News of failure, however, totally reverses the script. Disappointed with our own show of talent, we rush back to God to beg him to restore again our confidence and trust. A market *low* is always a stronger incentive to fold our hands in faith than a market *high*.

Prayer, as the last move of the desperate, is undoubtedly a religious act and worthy of divine attention, but is despair the best of reasons to initiate a dialogue with God? Aren't we courting the temptation that when dangers cease to threaten our security, our need for prayers will vanish?

Whatever role prayer assumes in times of storm or harmony, whatever relief it offers to the miserable or dejected, it is never allowed to be a substitute for the incapacity to love. To say "I pray for you" because I cannot say "I love you" is nothing but a pious charade. The very moment we stop loving, we stop praying; and when an icy heart moves our lips to petition, we make of prayer a useless gesture which neither God nor man accepts. "Yahweh, hear the plea of virtue, listen to my appeal, lend an ear to my prayer, my lips free from dishonesty" (Ps 17:1).

Prayer is not at its best when it remains on the sidelines of events; it belongs at the center of life. If it is allowed to influence our decisions and become the roots of our deeds, prayer undoubtedly would be at its happiest. As a historical cliché to mourn our heroes or bring propriety to important sessions, prayer is weakened in value. But to use prayer as a sedative for accepting and prolonging social injustices is the reversing of prayer's greatest mission: one of love and equality.

Prayer acknowledges no boundaries imposed by time and circumstances; it serves in fearful times as well as in times of tranquillity. Tortured prisoners seek its consolation in their distress, and silent nuns chant their psalms at daybreak in joyful search for God. "I will go before you levelling the heights. I will shatter the bronze gateways, smash the iron bars. I will give you the hidden treasures, the secret hoards, that you may know that I am Yahweh, the God of Israel, who calls you by your name" (Is 45:2–3).

The person who boasts that he never prays is either ignorant or conceited. Ignorance will excuse but pride demands a price. The proud one shouts thoughtlessly to the God who came to serve, "I do not serve!" With such a bold statement, man declares war on God, losing the battle before the fight begins.

Sometimes we flee from God simply because we cannot bear our own image. Irritated with ourselves, we become disenchanted with the one who caused this self to be. Complaints are heard instead of hymns of gratitude.

A nation that honors prayer sets standards for its people which augurs well for the future. When prayer is ignored or rejected, a decline of moral values is encouraged. If it is true that prayer is man's most noble act, what is true of a man who prays no more? Does a person without prayer really differ much from an animal? Tennyson says it well: "For what are men better than sheep or goats/That nourish a blind life within the brain,/If, knowing God, they lift not hands of prayer/Both for themselves and those who call them friend?"*

In our own country, one of the strongest on earth, public prayers are outlawed for the sake of separating Church and State even though God is deeply enshrined in the hearts and minds of our people. Prayer as a private function was never affected by legislation, but as a demonstrative act of public worship it was eliminated by law. Our schools, where youth are educated for the task of building the future, are run without benefit of the greatest book on earth. Isn't this precipitating a real danger in order to avoid a fictitious

* *Idylls of the King,* "The Passing of Arthur," ll. 418–421.

one? By withholding from our young people the moral values which prayer instills, we expose them to the fallacies of their nature uncurbed by laws of good and evil. The jungle that now reigns in many of our schools should be enough warning to alter our way of thinking.

Where is our godless society heading? Will the God who is not invited into the life of our younger generation be patient enough to remain with them in spite of rejection? Will he abandon his people as some secretly desire and hand us over to our own idolatries?

No one can answer these fateful questions; divine decisions are a mystery. The disturbing signs, however, which are so visible in every walk of life, should alert even the least thoughtful ones amongst us. Not to know when it is getting too late has brought evil days to many a nation. "He builds a nation up, then strikes it down, or makes a people grow, and then destroys it. He strips a country's leaders of their judgement, and leaves them to wander in a trackless waste" (Jb 12:23–24).

A spiritual vacuum seems to have spread over our many lands once called Christendom: a religious drought affects a territory as wide as the world. Prayerful customs and meaningful devotions, once the heart of religious fervor, have been gradually eliminated and replaced with nothing. Less and less of our time belongs to God while more and more of it is taken for ourselves.

The potentially honest ones are the first who realize that they are empty. Yearning for a deeper relationship with God, they refuse to drift along without ideals. If the God of Christianity is removed from their horizon, other deities will quench their incessant thirst. The moment the Christian West fails to provide the challenge sought, the gurus from the East will capitalize on the opportunities and attempt to fill the void.

Today, Eastern prayers and Eastern meditation receive much more than poetic curiosity, and the end of their popularity is not yet in sight. Cults of sometimes doubtful reputation are eagerly swelling the numbers of their disciples. Followers are recruited not only from those who fall easily for novelty but also from our better men and women who fail to recognize the beauty and depth of what they once considered holy. Those who depart from their faith surrender convictions they never came to know. "God is our shelter, our strength, ever ready to help in time of trouble, so we shall not be afraid when the earth gives way, when mountains tumble into the depths of the sea" (Ps 46:1–2).

Prone as human nature is to complain, we are quick to grumble against some arrangements made in heaven. We pray for a family and the cradle remains empty; we beg to keep good health and illness arrives; we work very hard and success never comes. Is God really listening? What is wrong up there?

We must remember that God is not impressed with haste. He has time and he takes it. With him as with nature, the seed must have time to grow.

When we insist on an immediate Yes or No, we might ruin what often needs time to blossom. A joy long desired and at last achieved brings greater satisfaction than wishes granted in a moment. God expects of us something which is in short supply in this instant age: perseverance, the tenacity to hold on to a petition and not let loose until the wish is granted. Saintly Monica repeated for so many years the request of her whole life: "Bring back to me, Oh Lord, my child." Again and again she stormed heaven without receiving a reply. Yet she never gave up, never lost hope. St. Augustine acknowledged her perseverance. "Nine years were to follow in which I lay tossing in the mud of that deep pit and the darkness of its falsity, though I often tried to rise and only fell the more heavily. All that time this chaste, god-fearing and sober widow— for such You love—was all the more cheered up with hope. Yet she did not relax her weeping and mourning. She did not cease to pray at every hour and bewail me to You, and her prayers found entry into Your sight.*

Many of us who strongly believe in God are exasperated by the monotony of continued prayers that seem to go unheard. We feel we did what was requested. We persevered in our petitions to God, we prayed again and again with little or no response. Can we be blamed if we think that God is too busy to be concerned with our small demands? We knocked at the door as Christ suggested, and the door remained closed, for weeks, months, years. We asked and we did not receive; yet God still expects us to be in love with him!

Those of us who are more tolerant of God's ways know our prayers are always answered, but that sometimes the answer is No. Why do we feel that God should never say No? Isn't it the right and duty of every parent to say either Yes or No to the child when the child is not in a position to know what is conducive

---

* *The Confessions of St. Augustine*, translated by F. J. Sheed (New York: Sheed & Ward, 1943), III: 11.

to proper growth? To be lovingly contradicted is love
at its best. "Indeed, I know it is as you say: how can
man be in the right against God? If any were so rash as
to challenge him for reasons, one in a thousand would
be more than they could answer" (Jb 9:2).

The power of prayer cannot be weighed. As our
most spiritual activity, it wings its way beyond all con-
cepts of limitations. Like any ruler it comes without
invitation and leaves without warning. Often it will
follow exactly the sequence of our thoughts and leave
at the very moment peace is achieved within ourselves. Ruled or unruled, we can never predict its
course.

There are particular moments in the day when God
must like to be with us: sunrise and sunset. The morning, representing the beginning of life, should be
opened with a blessing, and the evening which reminds us of the end of our days should close with a
hymn of gratitude. If God is faithfully invited to share
the happenings of our days and years, he will not be
very far away when life itself changes into what it will
be forever. If our last words on earth are a prayer, how
can we lose? If our last words on earth are a curse, how
can we win?

There was an old man in Jerusalem whose name was
Simeon. He was upright and devout. One wish kept
this holy man alive, to live long enough to see Christ,
his Lord. So he went up to the Temple to await his
dream, and the greatest moment of his life arrived.
Christ had been born and was brought to the Temple
by his parents. Simeon took Christ into his arms and
blessed God, saying, "Now, Master, you can let your
servant go in peace, just as you promised; because my

eyes have seen the salvation which you have prepared for all the nations to see, a light to enlighten the pagans and the glory of your people Israel" (Lk 2:29–32).

We are what we are before the eyes of God. If our life seeks strength in honest prayers, we can be trusted to serve others with nobility. Faithful to the promises made to God, we will be faithful to the promises made to man. Prayer and trust are welded together just as a heart is one with the gift of love.

If it is true that an entire ocean is affected by the power of a single river, how much more is the entire world affected by the power of a single prayer? A peaceful world is a longing shared by all of us. But how is this dream to be achieved? Can military strength alone provide stability on our shaky planet? Many put their total confidence in the power they yield and the money they control, only to find they can buy the voice of man but not his heart. Spiritual energies created by love and prayer are needed to heal the wounds and divisions of our world.

There is no heroism in declaring that spiritual values are out of style and moral precepts obsolete. But this "new morality"—which is neither new nor moral—leads humanity back again to the Darwinian struggle where only the strongest survive. The kind of life which grows on moral nihilism undermines all the hard-earned progress man has made in the past.

May we have the good sense to choose our leaders from the ranks of those who are intelligent, sincere, and humble in their dialogue with God! They alone deserve to wear the crown. "Whatever you undertake will go well, and light will shine on your path; for he that casts down the boasting of the braggart is he that saves the man of downcast eyes. If a man is innocent, he will bring him freedom, and freedom for you if your hands are kept unstained" (Jb 22:28–30).

Our nation's might is impressive when it is expressed in bombs, armor, and prosperity. We have wielded great influence on other nations because of the spiritual ideals on which our country was founded. Living standards enjoyed by no other nation make us the envy of the world. Even the moon is on the list of our conquered planets and many other stars arouse our curiosity. The power of the sun is being captured for use in building a better world. Today, we can project a future which could be the brightest mankind has ever seen. Or, perhaps, the darkest?

Are we content? Are we really satisfied with all the affluent superiority which so graciously cushions our lives? Is something lacking in the colorful parade of wonders? What is missing that should be there? What is the lost link that we do not talk about since we sense the shame of its absence. Is it prayer?

May it never happen that generations of the future, reflecting on our period of time, admire the way we conquered the world but deplored the price we paid for the loss of heaven.

chapter 5

MEDITATION . . . . .

the sea

Refresh me Lord, within my soul
As once you calmed the sea;
I sit and ponder blessedness
And search tranquillity.

In recent years, meditation and contemplation have climbed from the lowest peg of man's esteem to a considerably higher rating in appreciation and value. After a lapse of many decades, the civic community has discovered that the spiritual life is not just an outdated luxury for elderly religious but an integral part of human nature, without which the human potential will never reach fruition. Scientists too are curious and explore with surprising interest the effects of meditation upon the personality and character of human beings.

In current publications, men distinguished in science and philosophy readily admit that meditation exerts healing powers upon the nervous system of our highly pressured men and women. Meditation, in their view, is no longer identified with religious roots or pious inspirations. For them it is simply a noncultic effort to restore the inner harmony we have jeopardized in our chase for more and more material possessions.

Scientists and theologians both are aware of our instinctive hunger to adore a being greater than our dreams can ever fathom. Harried too long by a civilization which has left us painfully empty, we have grown tired of the security of the superficial and yearn to return home to the house of our father. Too hungry to look for bread we beg for peace. "I will leave this place and go to my father and say: Father, I have sinned against heaven and against you: I no longer deserve to be called your son" (Lk 15:18–19).

Three ways of reacting to a crisis are open to us: acceptance, refusal, or flight. If we are interiorly free, we will accept the challenge with all of its consequences, responsibilities, and inherent sacrifices. Painful as it might be, acceptance stimulates in us the energies which eventually bring us to peace.

If the refusal of the challenge is our choice, discontent becomes our master, and discolors life with envy and frustrations. Since no one likes to admit that he is too weak to face the difficulties life presents, he distances himself from the challenge in order to restore self-confidence.

The least honorable way to face a trial is to take to flight and leave to others the responsibility and agony of decision. Flight, which rarely reflects a hero, can be pardoned by the inability to see the need for action, but it is questioned when cowardice makes the decision.

Rightly conceived, meditation rallies the powers of acceptance and fosters uniting elements which bring us serenity and wisdom. Energies harvested in prayer and recollection not only support us on biological levels, like slowing down the heartbeat, alleviating a pressured respiratory rate, or lowering high blood pressure, but also inspire us in the spiritual realm, creating humility and trust. "Those who fear the Lord keep their hearts prepared and humble themselves in his presence" (Si 2:20).

Like many other mental activities, meditation and contemplation need certain conditions for growth and survival. Quiet surroundings head the list. Inner storms should be silenced and noise exiled from the boundaries of the soul. The manner should be calm and tranquil as we approach the prayer of reflection, otherwise prayers are not more than idle chatter.

No one claims, however, that even the best of our prayers will eliminate hardship and failure—no power is strong enough to achieve such wonder—but through the strength of prayers we can live with discords in harmony.

If we allow our Lord to find us, we can be alone with him wherever we may be. Mountains, seas, and deserts offer quiet places filled with the majesty of the divine. God's powerful mind, illuminating the distant horizons, strikes wherever it pleases, at any hour of the day, at any moment of the night. The instant, however, when God becomes our master, we sense very clearly that we are only travelers in time, looking for the endless day of heaven. "I have selected my servant David and anointed him with my holy oil; my hand will be constantly with him, he will be able to rely on my arm" (Ps 89:20–21).

Another aid in our pilgrimage to the holy mountain is our readiness to accept a message without opposing it for the sake of opposition. To enjoy a masterpiece without taking it apart the very moment we feel challenged is a grace bestowed on the self-controlled. Constraining as it may be, we all must learn the art of listening. Growth requires an inner space that allows room for new ideas to be molded. None of us is wise enough to answer all questions nor strong enough to fight our individual storms alone. There are times when our minds must change to furrows in the winter, eagerly awaiting the precious seeds of springtime. Four seasons God has granted and four seasons are needed to produce the riches of a harvest. Events arise in which passivity must yield to action to settle issues even at the cost of battle and to defend our freedom at the expense of war. "Do not suppose that I have come to bring peace to the earth: it is not peace I have come to bring, but a sword" (Mt 10:34).

No war, however, claims a right to stand alone. Only as a harbinger of lasting peace does it justify its pain-filled role in history. As soon as strife exhausts its fuel and reason conquers passion, the helmet of the warrior must vanish and the search for peace commence.

Meditation requires the attention of all the capacities at our disposal. Mind and body, diverse in their assignments, must learn to concentrate on one idea and focus on a single prayer. One truth, understood and assimilated, exerts far greater strength on our character than many ideas heard and forgotten. Knowledge, no matter how extensive, is never enough to satisfy our yearnings; emotions, too, must play their part in our growth to fullness.

A message understood must be experienced interiorly to achieve its full impact on our souls. The heart has its reasons of which reason is not always sure. Step by step, one idea experienced creates a base of strong conviction from which maturity takes its beginning. If we are urged always to say what we really mean, who could better fulfill this difficult demand than a man who meditates? "When in trouble I sought the Lord, all night long I stretched out my hands, my soul refusing to be consoled. I thought of God and sighed, I pondered and my spirit failed me" (Ps 77:2–3).

Many of us experience the intimacy which spiritual powers and physical strengths exert on each other. Nature well rested and disciplined provides a stronger vehicle for God's inspiration than nature exhausted or destroyed. One familiar with meditation will agree that a comfortable sitting position is important in order to create a favorable atmosphere. A good meditation presupposes a relaxed meditator, free from any strain or coercion imposed on the mind by the bodily posture.

The Christian tradition is generous and flexible in its concern for people: kneel, sit, stand, walk, or lie down. None of these positions is frowned upon; practically any position will do if it encourages the individual to initiate a more effective dialogue with the divine. If the kneeling position has survived for centuries, it was not because of divine revelation, but due to the conviction that kneeling was the humblest gesture in paying homage to the majesty of God.

Today, many of us prefer to stand in front of God and meditate with head slightly bowed, even though in the Eastern tradition of Hinduism and Buddhism the Lotus position is preferred. One sits on the floor, feet and ankles crossed in front, torso straight, arms hang-

ing loosely, relaxed. But it makes little difference how
we meditate and worship the divine, as long as we
have a *why* for our prayers. Only if meditation turns
into charades, with rituals and idols replacing sacrifice
and surrender, is God resentful of our gifts. To substitute the gesture for the spirit is a temptation we all
suffer when our desire for praise is stronger than our
faith in God. "And this became a pitfall for life, that
men, whether slaves to misfortune or princely power,
should have bestowed the incommunicable name on
sticks and stones" (Ws 14:21).

Most of our lives are shaped to a great degree by
powers set free through the mystery of incarnation.
After the coming of Christ, by his living and dying, he
set a pace which millions of people follow faithfully
and accept as the light and way which leads us into
our heavenly fulfillment. This ideal, however, standing before us like an unreachable star, has to come
alive in our particular situation with our own unique
limitations and our own individual characteristics and
personality. We all serve Christ one way or another,
but never in the same fashion. How much of the ideal
comes to life in our inner dimensions depends on the
way we let meditation influence our daily responsibilities. Whether we are people "inward bound" or
"outer directed" makes less difference than how we
use the sustaining support of these inner spiritual
forces.

If we are inclined to rely only on messages perceived and evolved by our analytical mind, which
probes, connects, and unifies, we will find ourselves
meditating rather than contemplating. In meditation,
we focus our intellectual curiosity on measureable

facts which are historically accepted and can be assumed as real: for instance, how we depend on God in our bodily and spiritual needs; how God sustains us and cares for us; and how we retaliate with our ingratitude and our sins. God's mercy is no doubt remembered, and there will always be God's forgiveness. But will the story of the prodigal son be ours when we return at life's greatest hour, the hour of our death?

In contemplation we assume the less active role of viewing the divine drama, like spectators who watch a performance on the stage. We see God more than we scrutinize him. God becomes a picture to behold rather than a puzzle to be solved. Reasons for existence are questioned with greater intensity than existence itself. Things are accepted on an immediate level without interpretation or explanation. With less reliance on discursive thinking, contemplation settles on inner understanding, seeing reality with inner energies rather than the light of mind.

Contemplation is not flight from reality; it is concentration perceived and valued in its true perspective. The best and worst in us is discovered, but not without the radiant aspects so often hidden and forgotten in the struggle of life. Only after discovering the eternal in others have we any hope to recognize the eternal in the heavens above. "Contemplation is not the pleasant reaction to a celestial sunset nor is it the perpetual twitter of heavenly birdsong. It is not even an emotion. It is the awareness of God, known and loved at the core of my being."*

* *The Cloud of Unknowing,* translated into modern English with an introduction by Clifton Wolters (Baltimore, Md.: Penguin Books, 1961), p. 36.

Technopolis, the city which emerged from giant mixers of concrete and steel, begs desperately to be released from its own embrace. Icy pavements support man's loneliest steps, leading him into an isolation in which he is apt to lose faith and hope. The divine command *to love our neighbor as we love ourselves* has been muted by another postulate: *Let us love each other or all of us will perish.* An order of God becomes a necessity of man.

For the sake of survival, we have to begin again to relate to each other and take into account what others yearn for. The ego alone cannot rule as master but must turn into a friend who is solicitous of the stress and tensions suffered by others. Well-intentioned aims of social workers will never suffice to alter the complexities of man's predicament. To bind a wound is not the same as healing it in its roots. Much stronger motives are called for if we are really going to lighten the burdens which distress the human family. Even with physical hungers stilled, the inner cravings of men in crisis have to be reckoned with, and whatever love and concern is needed to quiet their suspicions must be provided lest they perish in their need.

Meditation inspires a climate in which the atmosphere of trust can develop. To discover God in his majesty and disown man in his misery is too great a contradiction. Finding God must remain forever the prelude for the next step: the discovery of Man. To search for one without the other is tantamount to failure.

Divine goodness is reflected in earthly goodness, and faith unites where unbelief can only separate. Attractions to the beauties of creation stimulate a fascination for the beauty of the Creator, just as a masterpiece exalts the name of the artist. To reveal the mysteries of the divine to people who yearn for them is the language heaven understands the best. Only when we refuse to share what God has entrusted to our care are we failing in our mission. Was not God himself asking us to show our love for him whom we cannot see by our love for those we can see? "And the King will answer I tell you solemnly, in so far as you did this to one of the least of these brothers of mine, you did it to me" (Mt 25:40).

How does a person who meditates appear to others? Just like anyone else. After all, suits and haircuts do not distinguish between an atheist and a believer. If there is a difference, it is purely interior, on a level which cannot be seen; it can only be felt. People successful in meditation reach peaks in the art of loving rarely attained by others. How can anyone go out to annoy or hurt another after meeting God in prayer? After all, people can flee from our presence but they can never flee from our prayers. Those for whom we pray grow so close to our heart that the stranger of yesterday becomes the friend of tomorrow. Aren't we inclined to hold anonymous ones as objects of anger? Whom do we dress up as soldiers to fight our battles in war, if not the unnamed strangers?

People known by numbers only can easily become the target of hostility, while people in whom we invest our hearts are easier to love. Those interested in meditation gradually change into the object on which they meditate. And to become more like Christ means that the meditator becomes stronger in perception and sensitivity to the wants of his friends and enemies. *The Cloud of Unknowing* stresses it well. "All who engage in this work of contemplation find that it has a good effect on the body as well as on the soul, for it makes them attractive in the eyes of all who see them. So much so that the ugliest person alive who becomes, by grace, a contemplative finds that he suddenly is different, and that every good man he sees is glad and happy to have his friendship."*

Meditation must undergo the test of confrontation to prove itself worthy of all the confidence invested in it. The meditator is not exempt from temptations which tear into him without regard for virtue or immunity. The human animal can never be so domesticated that it rises beyond the danger of such assaults. Is anyone ever so holy that passions lose their sweetness and attractions. Can sanctity be declared sinlessness?

Light and darkness not only rush the pointers of time but also determine the distance from the heart of God. St. Augustine is only one of many who went through nightmares of defeat; memories of his dramatic struggle are kept alive in our minds as echoes of our own dilemma.

Nobility of birth bestows prerogatives in history but fails to secure favors in the eyes of our Lord. The elite cannot reserve parade grounds before the seat of judgment; it is here that equality is finally achieved. What unites us all is our weakness, not our strength. If anyone seems a little better off than another, it is the humble one who thinks of himself as little while God thinks of him as great.

If we admit that we have failed, without embellishing our guilt, we will not lose God, as we might fear, but will find him in his pardon and love him in his

* Ibid., p. 117.

mercy. Only those who bask in safety and consider themselves beyond reproach are the ones who must be warned against the dangers of complacency. "Meditation for them is, as it were, the sudden recognition and groping awareness of their own wretchedness, or God's goodness. This sudden perception and awareness is better learned from God than man. I do not mind at all if you, at this stage, have no other meditations upon your own wretchedness than such as come through the single word *sin* or *God*."*

We can never give more to each other than our love. If we love, we offer really all we possess. To ask for something in return is purely the exchanging of gifts, which is as far from love as heaven is from earth. In the exchange of gifts, we merely transfer ownership; in the exchange of love, we transfer the power of affection. Let us not forget that mere exchanges stir little interest in heaven since there is no merit gained in a give and take. Love is a pure gift with no other thought in mind except giving. Love knows no returns. It travels generously through one-way streets, blushing when discovered, and hiding if forced to expose its face. God himself is eager for our gift of love just as we are eager for the love of others. As we are loved, so will our life be.

Love, the greatest gift on earth, has become a rare phenomenon in our sphere of values. Counterfeits and substitutes threaten its existence to an ever growing extent and intensity. More endangered than any other virtue it is attacked by our hunger for possessions and besieged by our thirst for honors and glory. *Love me* has been debased to *Possess me*, and since possession

---

* *The Cloud of Unknowing*, p. 95.

is so alien to love, one contradicts the other. Far from bringing us together, possession often achieves the opposite effect.

Riches can only establish an external union providing a foundation too frail to sustain the burdens man must endure to master fate. But let us assure those who conclude with the help of computers that love is slowly dying that they have made errors in their tabulations which history alone will be able to correct. Love will never die. It will survive all threats of annihilation long after its enemies have perished. A world ruled by hate alone is earth's own hell, and if the hate leads to another hell hereafter, who can endure the thought! "No one who has been begotten by God sins; because God's seed remains inside him, he cannot sin when he has been begotten by God" (I Jn 3:9).

Meditation has the power to free our love from its chains since in its final analysis it purifies our thoughts and strengthens the motivation of giving. Selfish instincts ingrained in our souls as strong as tree roots can be uprooted if not redeemed by the strength of prayer and reflection. The impossible dream can be achieved by the gradual penetration of healing powers gained through contemplation and reflection. Inner stillness, permeating ever so slowly our wishes and desires, can cleanse our motivations, from which our convictions are born. Can avarice and greed survive in a climate where God is invited as a guest? Can night resist the powers of the sun?

By its very nature, meditation and reflection not only influence the shape of civilization, but also change the course of the lives of many of us who begin to see what was once beyond our understanding.

A new birth was recently announced in the continuing struggle for peace of mind: transcendental meditation (TM). Taking the bows are mysterious gurus with colorful turbans and difficult names. Arriving with headlines and a gentle message, the movement refuses any connection with organized religion. The technique of transcendental meditation attempts to challenge the creative intelligence of the man searching for harmony. It calls for the attention of the many and has already attracted quite a few.

A code of ethics based on natural laws is important to the disciples of TM. Happiness is pursued by earning the esteem of others, not by ordering it through authority or promise. Human potentials are awakened to full consciousness by total concentration, enabling the meditator to better adapt to the stress of modern living. To let the good within shine out is the goal of all efforts, the end result of all disciplines. New as TM seems to be, it is as old as Christian meditation. Basically, it is merely reviving some of the treasures we Christians allowed to fall asleep.

If TM would reveal more of its early roots and hide less of the meaning of the Mantra, it would make a contribution less difficult to accept. We have no intention to erect any barriers where they do not exist, nor are we in the mood to foster unfounded suspicions. However, no one can blame us for entertaining questions in an area where doubts linger and diminish our enthusiasm. Patience and understanding are needed if Christian meditation and transcendental meditation are to complement each other. "Treat me tenderly, and I shall live, since your Law is my delight. Shame seize the arrogant who defame me, when I meditate on your precepts!" (Ps 119:77–78).

chapter 6

HOPE . . . . .

the dawn

Each new day brings joy and pain
With hope to struggle on;
I stand with trust before you Lord
And seek another dawn.

Whenever we step over the line that others have drawn as ultimate and impassable, we step into the land of hope. When we allow undue caution or momentary adversity to break our spirit of adventure, we become a spectator instead of an explorer. The courage to create new frontiers is lost and the set boundaries are acknowledged as final.

Hope is trustful longing, the strongest link between reality and possibility. It challenges man to reach beyond himself, to dare to accomplish what others discard as impossible. To the hopeful person, every reasonable opportunity that life presents is a call that must be answered Yes or No because otherwise, the very opportunity ignored could be the one to make a difference.

A plus or minus sign on the pages of a ledger can be easily understood, but when it comes to a summary of our contributions we are really never sure how much we have added to life and how much we have taken away. The business man looks at the bottom line while we look into our conscience. How many will question their riches and how many will question their honesty?

Should we ever be definite about our limitations, beyond which we dare not step? Isn't the so-much-and-not-more reasoning only an excuse for not trying harder? When is the real moment of knowing that we have reached the outer limit of our effort? "Put up with your share of difficulties, like a good soldier of Christ Jesus" (II Tm 2:3).

Our being was not given to us as a readymade masterpiece just to be enjoyed and secretly admired. Life was accorded us as a mission to be fulfilled, a task to be mastered. What is handed on to us is the unfinished mystery, a lifetime of secrets waiting to be discovered. Those who expect from life fulfillments that were never promised are the ones most disappointed.

Life puzzles us with mysteries more easily recognized than solved. Ignorance can excuse us for not finding better solutions, but a pessimism that hampers our relationship with the world we live in is unpardonable. Who can be creative or have initiative in such a defeatist mood? Such a person is without hope—he is the one who will capitulate to the inevitable strains which hope would easily overcome.

Ego-complacency, on the other hand, can equally defeat the adventurous spirit of creativity. A person absorbed with his own importance measures everything to his own advantage. For him, God's variety and beauty implanted in our universe shrinks to the tiny measure of his own ego.

More damaging than either pessimism or complacency is the feeling of inferiority. Lack of hope in one's self badly impairs any effectiveness. The mentality that apologizes too quickly for personal actions shies away from the exposure to failure and refuses any responsibility that might arise. No situation should ever be considered as beyond hope of change, since every situation in life must be passed through and outgrown so that we can reach the promise of a better tomorrow. *Death from Lost Hope* becomes the epitaph on the tombstone of such lost opportunities.

Hope is at its best when we are prepared at any moment to accept what life has in store for us, pleasant or not, and to keep our balance if the long-awaited dream falls short of expectations. True hope keeps the mind open and alert without depending on immediate fulfillment. Our confidence remains healthy despite temporary setbacks.

To hope for something that can never be, however, is senseless. The impossible dream, entertained too long, can make us strangers in our own land. Genuine hope focuses only on what can possibly be achieved.

Hope and youth beget each other. No one whose hope is vibrant can feel old or useless. Those who are fortunate enough to remain mentally alert and buoyant while enjoying the fruits of long experience are the ones who know life at its best. "Planted in the house of Yahweh, they will flourish in the courts of our God, still bearing fruit in old age, still remaining fresh and green, to proclaim that Yahweh is righteous, my rock in whom no fault is to be found!"(Ps 92:13–15).

The message of hope means even more to the old than to the young. The closer we move to the boundaries of the unknown, the more we call upon hope to quiet our apprehensions and support our courage. Old age tends to bring disillusion about the emptiness of earthly promises. Having heard so much and seen so little, the elderly finally turn to the ultimate source of all our hopes, Christ. With hope in his promises and faith in his Way and his Truth, their last years become a time of marvelous discovery. Without such hope and faith, what is left to them?

In those who live only in the past—if they live at all—the loss of hope is evident. When all one's energies are spent exploring the memories of yesterday, with little or no enthusiasm left for the present, one is already in the world of the forgotten. To stop living while still alive, to refuse to let our personality grow richer is to surrender to the enemy within us. Using the yesterday as a defense against the tomorrow is admitting to oneself "I am less of a man than I was years ago."

Unless hope is active in us, there will be little effective planning or action on our lives. Those who awaken each morning with the sad conviction that nothing makes any difference, and who end the day with a stronger conviction that nothing *has* made any difference, will surely not stir themselves to any decisive action. Instead of being ready at every moment to receive what is yet to come, they are willing to condemn to death what is not yet born. Not only nascent life can be aborted, but also ideas, plans, and the grace of hope. "O death, your sentence is welcome to a man in want, whose strength is failing, to a man worn out with age, worried about everything, disaffected and beyond endurance"(Si 41:3–4).

Man, often the dreamer, aspired to walk on the moon. Our times, times of hope, achieved this greatest of technical wonders. The moment our spaceman took his first cautious step on the surface of the moon, hope was vindicated, hope had stepped over the impassable line.

Not all of us are called upon to explore the moon, but isn't there at least a little star in our sky that awaits our personal discovery? Not having the ability to be a hero does not excuse us from trying to perform as well as we can.

Is not idleness of mind and the ensuing boredom at the root of our failures more often than we care to admit? When we blame others for obstructing our progress, are we not, instead, indicting ourselves for refusing a challenge before we really face it?

Lack of character and of will makes its appearance in strange and contradictory ways. All too often the strongest expression of the weakest is to destroy. Some set a building afire to forget that they are too feeble to spark a flame in their own souls. Others tear down reputations since anything diminished makes them appear greater by comparison.

As words, *hope lost* may sound quite innocent. As a reality, however, it can take tragic turns, flaring into violent action. Not that we deny the fact that all of us have contradictory elements in our makeup, but those who have nothing to lose are usually the ones who are best at destruction.

We all have the duty to disclose what we really are. During our lifetime we confess not only to God but also to our family and friends whether we have lived up to our potential or shirked our responsibilities. Whatever the verdict—good, bad, or indifferent,—it will never be final. Just as evolution spurs natural forces, so do our inner riches also evolve. No one remains the same over a lifetime. We advance or step back, often unsure of either direction. In less honorable moments we abandon our duties and leave to others the burdens that are rightly ours; in our nobler moments we move beyond our own frontiers to master the exceptional. And always we are called upon to meet what fate presents; only death should be allowed to bring our forward motion to a halt.

The most beautiful human experience is in seeking transcendence. Mind and soul are forever yearning for what is beyond. Somehow we know that there is more of life than what the *now* provides: a life so radiant that even St. Paul, who caught a glimpse of the eternal, could find no words to do justice to its magnificence. "It is a wisdom that none of the masters of this age have ever known, or they would not have crucified the Lord of Glory; we teach what scripture calls: *the things that no eye has seen and no ear has heard, things beyond the mind of man, all that God has prepared for those who love him*" (I Co 2:8–9).

God leads us in various stages from promise to fulfillment. As a God of promise, he announces the coming of glory at a time he will choose. To trust this promise and, in hope, to anticipate it now, is the faith we must keep on earth. The more we orient our lives according to the Gospel, the stronger will be our hopes in the eternal kingdom. If we are truly convinced that there is a future in Christ, how can we mind sharing our present times with him?

The promise of the new heaven and new earth must take precedence when other more self-centered longings try to influence our actions. Christian hope, which is openness for the always more relevant God, inspires us to a surrender that knows only one beginning and one end: Jesus Christ, who suffered, died, and rose on the third day to ascend into heaven.

Yet Christian hope is not so strongly attached to heaven that it cannot move freely on earth. It expresses itself, not in rest with angels and saints, but in restlessness among the sinners of earth. It is not passive waiting for the moment when heaven's doors will open, but creative action in the present, to earn the heavenly reward. The glory promised gives us the incentive to transform this world of ours into a more just and peaceful home.

To proclaim God's wisdom without being concerned for man's folly is far from the fullness of Christian love. We do not wish to flee from our suffering brothers and sisters but to heal their afflictions while we are with them, and to point the way to Christ. Only when Christian hope reacts as responsibly toward God as toward man is it genuine and holy. "Yahweh, my heritage, my cup, you, and you only, hold my lot secure; the measuring line marks out delightful places for me, for me the heritage is superb indeed. I bless Yahweh, who is my counsellor, and in the night my inmost self instructs me; I keep Yahweh before me always, for with him at my right hand nothing can shake me" (Ps 16:5–8).

Hope, in its very roots, carries tensions into our lives which test our patience. Our hope for heaven and our way on earth often run in opposite directions, setting one against the other. The open or hidden conflicts strain our relationship with God. Those who do not hear the inner alarms remain undisturbed and continue to live as if earth alone exists. Those, however, who are fully alive to their inner warnings will feel the discord and strive for a harmonious balance.

To survive on a greedy earth, hope needs support from a suffering God. Crucifixion, inseparable from resurrection, was an integral part of salvation. Nailed to the cross, Christ paid the price a sinful earth demanded, but as risen Savior he proved that hope is ever the victor. The cross is a powerful symbol of hope reminding us that despair must never be the last act in the drama of life. With Christ, we accept our share of the human burden, convinced that heaven is waiting.

Christ's future, which is mankind's future, will find its completion when the final transformation of the world takes place. Then Christ will be "everything in every thing," hope and faith will merge with love, and love alone will reign. At last our nights will perceive the dawn. "This I believe: I shall see the goodness of Yahweh, in the land of the living. Put your hope in Yahweh, be strong, let your heart be bold, put your hope in Yahweh" (Ps 27:13–14).

A different hope has arisen in our era, the hope which atheistic materialism promises to a hungry mankind. Powerful in many lands and tightly organized in many political structures, it promises a hope totally contained within material boundaries. With heaven emptied of its God, nothing remains but an earthly promise of a classless society in which everything supposedly gives according to capacities and receives according to needs. But to achieve this paradise on earth, violence is condoned—not the violence against oneself sanctioned by Christ but the violence against others who are declared enemies of the new society.

These two kinds of hope, as different as can be, are now locked in a contest too intense to end in a draw. For us to wait for God's cause to succeed without a wholehearted effort on our part to correct prevailing injustices, is a strange way to prepare for a showdown. To beseech heaven to let our enemies fail without actively trying to cure the causes that brought their enmity into existence is a prayer that God will never hear. Defeat is no more avoided by claiming God as our invincible partner than success is achieved by wishful thinking. Only when faith and justice have become prevalent enough to influence the mind and soul of man can victory be ours. Until that day arrives, we live a precarious existence, and those who expect effortless tranquillity must wait for the arrival of some future century. "It is not those who say to me, 'Lord, Lord', who will enter the kingdom of heaven, but the person who does the will of my Father in heaven" (Mt 7:21).

How many of us allow hope to participate fully in the vital decisions that determine the course of our life? Is hope for us only a generalized theme applying to humanity as a whole but having no particular reference to our individual existence? Is it a virtue that we only pray for but forget to live?

Our social and moral difficulties are increasing at an incredible pace. Fear and violence demand their victims in ever-growing numbers. Our globe, so small in the eyes of moon-faring astronauts, is being torn apart by vicious conflicts of bodies, minds, and hearts.

Is all humanity stricken with blindness at the very moment that sight is so desperately needed? Have we lost our reason just when sound judgments are required? The clues are there for us to see and hear in the warning voices of historians, sociologists, psychologists, and above all in the voices of the messengers of the word of God.

When will we be ready, when will we be willing to follow our star? "When I saw him, I fell in a dead faint at his feet, but he touched me with his right hand and said, 'Do not be afraid; it is I, the First and the Last; I am the Living One'" (Rv 1:17).

Hope is our last and strongest weapon. Firmly rooted in the promises of a living God, it can still turn our present chaos into a prelude of a reign of peace and justice. Without this hope and the effort it inspires, a masterless night in which terror roams unchecked will annihilate the best of our dreams. The one who surrenders is the one who is lost.

chapter 7

HUMILITY . . . . .

the universe

How great your universe, Oh Lord
How small this heart of mine;
Humbly do I follow you
To live your gift of time.

Humility is truth. If we truly accept ourselves as we are, we are humble. The moment we root our security in the soil of our own individuality, we are genuine in character and true to our personality.

To submit to the demands of humility, the greatest of all virtues, is to submit to laws which are immanent to our nature. If we refuse to adorn our crown with stolen values and reject the urge to embellish our name with treasures earned by another, we unveil the being God conceived when he created us.

Full experience of our talents and complete acceptance of our limitations are conditions necessary if life is to be real and honest. There is no place for the lie. Self-exaltation is a hostile element in the growth of our personality just as self-abasement delays the discovery of the real. Natural abilities which enrich the human life are not to be denied. They must be graciously accepted as gifts from God, who returns at journey's end to demand a strict account of our deeds. " 'Sir', he said 'you entrusted me with five talents; here are five more that I have made!' His master said to him, 'Well done, good and faithful servant; you have shown you can be faithful in small things, I will trust you with greater; come and join in your master's happiness'" (Mt 25:21–22).

The unreal never exists and the real never ceases to be. Imaginary greatness, unworthy compliance or blind dependence all destroy the strategy of the divine. Attempts of man to raise himself to the pinnacle of an absolute is to deny the real situation into which we were born and in which we must die. The temptation to discard God's intention in our life and put his script aside is very human. Nearly everyone has worked on a scheme in which God's role has been reduced to that of spectator. But to ask him to be an observer only, simply condoning our actions and blessing our deeds is belittling God's greatness.

How often have we planned the course of our days with little thought in mind but success at any price? Falsehoods, excuses, and pretensions are used to capitalize on goals which others have already achieved. The goal, to get as much as we can with the least expense, becomes an ideal for the many who see "success" as the only way in life.

Does God expect us always to succeed in our efforts? Has he ever identified defeat as shame? Throughout his years of public life, was not Christ himself plagued with failure and disappointment? Isn't it true that quite a few things went wrong in *his* career? Denials pursued him more often than approval. How frustrated he must have felt at being misunderstood by his own people, including the apostles who abandoned him in the crucial hours.

Well then, what counts in life if not success? What will have weight on our scales when God himself is ready to scrutinize the worth of our deeds? What will impress the One to whom the judgment is assigned? Will the points we consider as highlights be of any interest to God? Will great and small take a reversal at the hour of final accounting?

God's interest is focused on our stewardship. How have we brought our capabilities to bear on decisions where justice was at stake? How brightly was our light shining when darkness offered us a place to hide? How honest were we when dishonesty became a way of life accepted by so many? To fail with dignity is often better than to succeed with guilt, and only the man without fear will make the right decision.

The world is doing its level best, day and night, to make us act and think and speak alike. Conform and you will be welcomed; step out of the mold and you will be shunned. Fall into step with the march of others and you will never lose your way; be glad that you can be an echo and forget to be a voice. . . .

The allurement of popularity is pervasive. "Do what the others do" relieves us of the burden of responsibility and eliminates the risks which could bring discomfort into our life. "Play safe" becomes a new commandment so strictly kept that hardly anyone needs absolution. No right or wrong is tabulated in our conscience since all of us are safely hidden behind the mantle of obscurity. "He goes in search of words, but there are none to be had" (Pr 19:7).

Imitation exacts a bitter price: the surrender of self. Those who cherish inner treasures which cannot be bought will firmly chart their own course. Others without a personality of their own have nothing to lose and easily follow the instincts of the herd. The first strive for honesty, the others become imitators, while in between amble those who are too weak for either path.

Since we really possess only what we are from within, we are never poorer than when we give away what we are. With our spiritual center destroyed, what values can we offer to a world of hunger and expectation? Possessions stolen can be replaced, but when robbed of the self, where can we flee for consolation? Some will perish in the anger of frustration, never awakening to their loss. Others will survive with marks of degradation, never knowing what meaning life can really have.

When supported by spiritual wealth, the inner man will never totally surrender to the strings of the puppet. Once we have tasted our true identity, we cannot be content without it. Stronger than any physical pains are the pangs of spiritual desertion. There beats in all of us a remorse which begs forgiveness after betrayal. Where once we wished, in vain, to become so many men, we now dream to become one man: ourself.

This self, accepted and lived, strengthens forces within us which shape our character and determine our personality. What we have firmly under our control can readily be shared with others. With our being secure, we willingly dispense our wealth without the fear of loss. Love and generosity come almost naturally if we can face all threats to survival.

Humility, as a creative power, divides itself without ever sacrificing its potential. The gifts of the humble are rendered with one idea in mind: to help those who have less than we. No cleavage exists between giver and receiver; they are united by a grace which allows one to be generous and the other to be needy. No wonder humility and love are complementary forces in the development of spiritual maturity! Each is a hunger as each is a blessing. Which is the greater is difficult to discern. The one who gives, sensing satisfaction, becomes alerted to the dangers of possession, while the one in need is taught to see in acceptance an honor rather than a shame. "There must be no competition among you, no conceit; but everybody is to be self-effacing. Always consider the other person to be better than yourself, so that nobody thinks of his own interests first but everbody thinks of other people's interests instead" (Ph 2:3–4).

Identity is the one thing in life which has to be defended without a thought of capitulation. No threat or pressure from without should ever become so strong that we yield to its menace. To bear witness to the truth with full mind and heart is cause enough to withstand any bribe or compromise. Loss of life is better than betrayal. The immortal ones in the past who defied the threats of tyrants without hesitation paid the highest price for their personal convictions. Death was preferred to surrender. They left behind a heritage to be admired, if not imitated. They heroically defended what cowards were willing to give up to the highest bidder. How different the rewards each of them received for their performance. Our own generation, so often imitating the extremes, hides many an unsung hero who would not hesitate to defend what we consider holy and divine. "I take my stand on my integrity, I will not stir; my conscience gives me no cause to blush for my life" (Jb 27:6).

To convince others that humility is more fact than fiction, we must endure the test of life. If it is hard at times to prove our love for others, how much harder it is to prove humility! The face can wear so many masks it becomes difficult to see the real. Weakness, camouflaged as virtue, and cowardice, paraded as submission, often infiltrate the roots from which the virtue grows and blossoms. Humble talk and modest gestures will never prove that we are really humble. Responsibility for our actions and the resolve to keep a promise once made is what is expected. The world has grown skeptical of empty words thrown into the wind. Deeds alone speak the language best understood. "There is no room in my house for any hypocrite, no liar keeps his post where I can see him" (Ps 101:7).

Inner developments call for specific stages of maturity. If even one phase of growth is omitted, some degree of deformity ensues. The moment we acknowledge the real in us, we attain a comfortable level of social interaction which absolves us from the impulse of comparing ourselves to others. We recognize that we are equal in diversity, not better or worse than anyone else, and we find it natural to extend the same privilege to others. Secure in our position, applause is not essential and criticism is not rejected. With independence we make our choice in accordance with inner judgment, agitated as little by the sounds of victory as by the news of failure. Even courage loses its meaning, since nothing can be taken from our being.

The self, once established, can finally be traded in for the satisfaction of commitment. Christian faith, centering on deeds performed for others, stirs in us the desire to lose what we have found, not for the sake of emptiness but for the glory of fulfillment. By our actions we either give to others or take for ourselves. Neutrality does not exist. The less we are concerned with our own well-being, the more free we become for the demands of others. Only a fortified stronghold, a closed personality, has to be attacked in order to be taken.

With the needs for self-defense loosened, we become more receptive to those who have not yet found their way. Indifference is finally overcome in a world which accepts it without remorse or question. Non-commitment is replaced with care for those who are loved by God but ignored by man. Our lot is cast with the lowly ones, the ones so greatly considered in God's point of view.

All through Christian tradition we applaud the man who loses his life in order to find it, while we condemn the man who finds his life in order to lose it. We have been hearing this for centuries now, but does the thought really go beyond our ears? Our faith is threatened from all corners of the universe, and prophets of gloom see disasters crowding the horizon. Unknowingly, we add our own share of discontent by only believing, instead of living, the faith God gave to us.

God's message, which is so much the message of humility, has hardly touched the roots of our being. Religion has become more a prerogative of milieu, heritage, and upbringing than of inner fire, death, and resurrection. Events no longer take place; customs, ceremonies, and repetitions now fill our schedule to overflowing. Even martyrs are not needed, since they have lost their appeal for our generation. Our convictions, previously strong enough to withstand the temptations of our day, are now regulated by computers programed to public taste telling us what to do and when. "There is no cure for the proud man's malady, since an evil growth has taken root in him. The heart of a sensible man will reflect on parables, an attentive ear is the sage's dream"(Si 3:28–29).

Small ones must exist so that great ones can be measured. Often we have to destroy selfish desires so that God's creation can arrive at its full potential. Not too many people are courageous enough to allow this to happen, and fewer still will attempt to bear with all the consequences.

To live without a challenge of ideals, existing purely for the sake of existence, is the temptation of an age brilliant in its technical wonders yet poor in its moral convictions. Foreboding signs are flashing all around us. In ever-growing numbers we realize that something must be done to stem the tide of immorality and crime, but this requires the courage of conviction. Who really has it?

Isn't it much easier to trod the beaten path than to risk clearing a new way to light?

Since we are never pure humanity, we are never able to reach the peak of pure humility. Perfection in this virtue calls for complete self-surrender, involving the whole complexity of our personality. It does not seem to be in the nature of man to be the perfect master of his being. Escape routes are kept open and compromises sought which dilute a perfection Christ alone can claim. Vanity and glory stimulate our pride much

more than they encourage our humility. If we ask ourselves why we acted the way we did, the answer might
be so embarrassing we would prefer leaving it unsaid.

The only permanent element in our nature is our
willingness to struggle on, even if we suspect that we
are losing. To be daring enough to seek humility in
any conflict we encounter is all that we can offer as we
attempt to meet the expectations of the divine. This is
undoubtedly one of our greatest gifts to heaven.

Laws are written to establish order in our society,
while at the same time they maintain discipline and
justice in our dealings with self and others. Humility,
a basic law of humanity, establishes truth and honesty
in our relationship with God and man. Pride seriously
violates that law. We behave toward God indepen-
dently, forgetting that all we possess has been received through his kindness. Toward man, we act in a
dishonest way, as we pretend to be what we are not.

The definition of pride can be the same as the definition of our lies when we speak and act against our
better knowledge. Due to an inordinate desire for ex-
cellence, be it ever so fictitious, we consider ourselves
as our first beginning and our last end. There is a lot of
good in us, seen or unseen, dormant or alive. To enjoy
such goodness and bring it to perfection is the goal we
try so hard to reach. Often, however, during the heat of
the day, we become blinded to our dependence on
God and act as if we were our own masters without the
need of heaven. "The beginning of human pride is to
desert the Lord, and to turn one's heart away from
one's maker" (Si 10:14).

Pride renders useless everything it touches. Beautiful actions performed only for applause are worthless
in the sight of God. Accomplishments intended for

self-glory alone wither away before they are of any use to others. God shows little interest in anything from which he is excluded.

Remember the Pharisee? He knew Scripture by heart, tended meticulously to his religious obligations and kept the law with dedication and fervor. And God had no use for him. "Vanity they pursued, vanity they became" (Jr 2:5).

What the Pharisee did was for himself alone. His own glory outdistanced the glory of God. All activity prompted by a purely natural intention is deprived of God's cooperation and since grace is absent, life is missing. What remains is the empty shell, which is good enough for showmanship but hardly good enough for divine recognition. How disappointed the proud one will be if, after death, he finds himself without reward. Although he labored throughout life in God's vineyard, he will find it was done in vain.

To punish the proud, God has no need to arm himself with a sword; it is enough to leave the proud man to himself. Nothing is weaker than the man abandoned by the support of the divine. How desolate the world must look to him if it reflects only his selfish dreams. Dangers to the perils of existence which alert the humble are lost in the appraisal of the proud who say that God should stay busy with the play of angels, that it is the individual who is to rule his destiny alone. "The fool says in his heart, 'There is no God! Their deeds are corrupt and vile" (Ps 14:1).

Pride at its worst is seldom the problem that plagues the average Christian. The *non serviam*—I do not serve—of the rebellious angels, which merited immediate banishment to hell, is a rare experience in our life. The lighter portion, however, in which pride appears as conceit and arrogance, is too often an integral part of our daily diet. When we find the dialogue of others uninteresting or boring, we are apt to blame the inadequacy on the other person alone instead of looking to ourselves for the failure to understand. When we have a natural aversion to someone, are we rejecting the person or is it because our feelings are hurt by an intellect obviously sharper than ours? If we refuse a call to help another on the grounds of not feeling up to it, are we hiding fears of coming out second best? Whenever our advice is not accepted, do we sulk because our self-esteem is hurt and our wisdom questioned?

Do we still have to belittle others to feel great in our own sight? Must a mountain crumble to a mere mound so that we can reach the peak? Is our own way to fame paid for by the sacrifices and denials of others?

We need humility to say to the other, "You are great and I am not," just as we need freedom to let the other pass ahead if he deserves the higher rank. "The greater you are, the more you should behave humbly, and then you will find favour with the Lord" (Si 3:18).

And yet caution is advised before we declare a person's behavior as proud. Just as an exterior show of humility does not always indicate the presence of the virtue, an exhibition of arrogance does not always pass as vice or aberration. It happens more than we presume that a person afflicted with painful feelings of inferiority will assume an air of haughtiness to make up for deficiencies. Youthful quest for admiration is another reason for compensation in which attention is sought by outwardly refusing it. And don't we all, at times, claim a perfection which we never really possess?

Such self-deception is, without doubt, a sign of immaturity, but its roots are as innocent as boyish boasting. No harm is done by praising oneself in humor, if humor is sincere. A response of understanding and compassion is of greater help in such a case, rather than weary admonitions. The more reserved we are in judgment, the greater our influence will be. Beneath the outer rind of defiance we may discover depths of docility and a will to learn and listen. The selfless man will know the difference, and he should be chosen to tame the youthful fire.

Can mighty pride ever be conquered? Do we possess the courage to curb the elements that make pride our greatest sin? Are we strong enough to withstand the fury of the waves which pride stirs up on our shores? Can our motivations ever be pure enough to finish our task for the simple joy of accomplishment?

Alone, it will be hard to succeed. Prayers are needed: humble enough to assure us of the necessary graces of God. But something must be added to these prayers to prove that they are real—the willingness to accept humiliation as it comes. To ask God to make us humble and then curse him when we are tried is the unadulterated hypocrite in those of us who speak and act with contradiction.

Humility and pride confronted each other in a drama involving Christ, a sinful woman, and a Pharisee. Christ had been invited to the home of a Pharisee for dinner. As he took his place at the table, a woman with a bad reputation entered the house carrying a jar of ointment. She was weeping and her tears fell on the feet of Christ. With her hair, she wiped them away and anointed his feet with oils.

The observant Pharisee had his own ideas, thinking that if this man were a prophet, he would know what this woman was who was touching him and what a bad name she had. Our Lord, being more than a prophet, could see the goodness of the woman who knelt at his feet, just as he was conscious of the mentality of the Pharisee who judged himself above all miseries. With whom did God's sympathy finally rest?

Faced with moral weakness fully admitted and self-righteousness totally denied, Christ said to the Pharisee, " 'Her sins, her many sins, must have been forgiven her, or she would not have shown such great love. It is the man who is forgiven little who shows little love.' Then he said to her 'Your sins are forgiven' " (Lk 7:47–48).

God's decision was made, humility stood glorified and pride condemned. How differently the two antagonists must have returned home on this eventful day when they met their Lord and Master; one with a lesson learned, the other with a lesson lost.

Humility and pride are two vast movements which have deeply influenced the events of history. Strong as the winds of hurricanes and swift as the speed of missiles, they aim at heights so dazzling and sublime not even angels can resist their fascination. Inconspicuous in their beginning, humility and pride quickly establish their pervasive power and exert their pressure on many days of history. They never rest until all other powers have been drawn into their magnetic orbit. "I do not serve" is challenged by "Be it done to me according to thy wish," forcing all of us to take a stand between the greatest virtue and the greatest sin. If it is said that there is no sin of which pride is not the root, we can safely add that there is no virtue without humility claiming its part. Humility brought Christ to life, while pride condemned him to a cruel death. Awesome are the powers of the two.

There comes a time when everyone must disregard perfection and lay aside imagined virtue to reach a common level with those who feel inferior and poor. Distinctions kept alive to build up our image of propriety and honor must be destroyed before we meet the God who is always ready to exalt the lowly. The mask must fall before the fall of our curtain.

There comes the time when we are totally aware of our inevitable encounter with God who was so humble himself. There comes the time when we realize that what unites us all is not our strength, but our weakness.

Greatness will be ours if we dare to be humble, and small we shall remain if we pretend to be great.

chapter 8

OUR BODY . . . . .

the seed

And I, Oh Lord, spring forth from
* seed*
Which thou hast left behind
To strengthen with thy love and
* grace*
My body and my mind.

Spiritual and mental alertness is influenced to a decisive degree by the health of our body. If our physical
condition is sound and our energies vibrant, our
spiritual faculties prosper. If our body is fatigued, ill,
or listless, our mental and spiritual powers diminish.
Theologians remind us that grace builds on nature,
and it seems equally true that ideas depend on a
generous supply of vitality.

With the functions of mind and body so intimately
connected, with thinking and acting so dependent on
each other, shouldn't we question ourselves about
what our body means to us, what role it plays in our
life and how we respond to the demand it makes on
us?

What kind of relationships with our body can we
enter into? Are there options open to us which we can

accept or decline, or are we less in command than we like to think we are?

By being a little too casual about self-discipline, have we allowed our body to assume a control far beyond its right? Have we granted it, little by little, the power to dictate to us as a master dictates to a slave?

In such a case, physical needs assert themselves with such pressure that they overshadow other needs equally or even more essential to our total well-being. Our concern for food, drink, sleep, and other personal satisfactions become so insistent that nothing else can match their importance. Our emotions, even our fantasies and dreams, become so involved with corporeal hungers and thirsts that little attention is given to the stirrings of our mental and spiritual faculties. In the very core of our being, consciously or not, we identify with the ceaseless demands of our physical appetites and are rarely inspired to strive for the higher levels.

When the body is master, what affects it affects the whole self. Not only our corporeal being but our pride, honor, confidence, and self-acceptance are bound up with our physical fate. If our body is abused, we are completely subdued; our self-respect is pulled up by the roots. Identifying harm to our body with inflictions upon our soul, our injuries signal distress to our spirit.

Multiply this individual demoralization by thousands or even millions, and we can begin to understand the abject submission by the whole segments of mastered nations in our time. "A body dies when it is separated from the spirit, and in the same way faith is dead if it is separated from good deeds" (James 2:26).

If a person who is ruled by his body enters religious life, he will tend to favor ceremonies over meditation and visible penance over inner mortification. Exterior acts, observed and acknowledged, seem to be of greater value than hidden actions known to God and self alone.

Mastery by the body also influences the values which shape our personality. Material goods outrank spiritual wealth; what we actually are seems less important than what we possess; money, position, titles, degrees, outweigh ideas and wisdom. Power, translated into influence, is more of an asset than learning, and inner goodness is outclassed by a shrewdness that judges things according to profit rather than moral obligations. "My son, in the course of your life test your constitution, and do not allow it what you see is harmful to it; for everything does not suit everybody, nor does everybody take pleasure in everything. Do not be insatiable over any delicacy, do not be greedy over food, for overeating leads to sickness, and gluttony brings on biliousness. Many have died of gluttony; beware of this and you will prolong your life" (Si 37:27–34).

All this does not, of course, refer to those who, on rare occasions give in to the temptations of fine food and drink. Perfect control is not always within reach. Festivals and special happenings which enliven the monotony of our days are too precious to ignore even though for a little while they may threaten our healthy balance. But unremitting addiction to food and drink not only hurts our physical well-being but also diminishes our human dignity. To be fully alive only when we eat or drink reduces us to the animal level. "A little is quite enough for a well-bred person; his breathing is easy when he gets to bed. A moderate diet ensures sound sleep, a man gets up early, in the best of spirits" (Si 31:19–20).

As less disciplined people allow the body to become their master, those whose mind and will dominate the physical forces may go to the opposite extreme. The relationship between the self and the body becomes a hostile one: the body is declared an enemy. Physical desires are seen as inimical forces that must be beaten back and overcome. Needs of the flesh and those of the mind confront each other with an antagonism that makes it difficult to establish a stable meeting place. Sometimes the physical stirrings are simply disregarded and left unserved; at other times they are smothered with a determination that approaches fanaticism. The mind hardly rests until the bodily urges are totally subdued.

In a person whose mind rules the body, the reaction to physical harm is of a different nature than when the body rules. Indignities to the flesh harm only the flesh; they do not damage the integrity of the inner self. Indeed, often the afflictions strengthen one's courage to bear them. Not only our early Christians, who defied Caesar and faced death in the arena, but countless brave men and women in the intervening centuries and in our own day have proved that the human spirit can triumph over physical agony. "Do not be afraid of those who kill the body but cannot kill the soul; fear him rather who can destroy both body and soul in hell" (Mt 10:28).

When the mind is hostile to the body, one who worships the sacred will tend to seek expression in inner performance known only to God. The ceremonies that are integral to our liturgy and devotions are respected but not considered indispensable. The soul's silent adoration is preferred to prayers formed by the lips alone.

This inimicable relationship between mind and body can be tempered to a degree that brings us a certain beneficial independence. Such a choice means an austere mode of living which, however, provides opportunity for one's mental capacities to develop in unusual freedom.

Hostility, even though tempered, between mind and body will not lead to the ideal relationship. The radical domination of spirit over flesh is achieved by a dangerous split in the personality, and can be kept up only by continual disregard of values which we need to keep our humanity intact. Unfeeling replaces feeling, harshness replaces warmth, while absorption in our own internal battle leaves little room or sensitivity for the needs of the rest of humanity.

Some may consider it heroic to disregard or deny the body, God's greatest natural gift to us; but is it really so impressive an achievement to destroy a natural balance in which body, mind, and spirit work in amicable cooperation? Eastern asceticism of the type practiced widely in India and China emphasizes the point.

In their stern mortification of bodily desires, Hindus and Buddhists reflect a strong hostility to material needs and physical comforts, as well as to the warmth of personal relationships. In their view, the body, with its violent and illicit impulses, is something to be endured only. The spiritual sky has to be man's roof, but his body, the material tent, is accorded no value. In the Isopanisad we read: "One should always remember that as long as he has a material body he must face the miseries of repeated birth, old age, disease, and death. There is no use in making plans to get rid of these miseries of the material body. The best course is to find the means by which one may regain his spiritual identity."*

The Christian understanding of self-control is of quite a different order. It maintains a healthy balance between the needs of the spirit and the hungers of the flesh. With no tension between mind and body, the whole person enjoys the inner freedom to establish a cooperative relationship between the two.

And this leads us to the third option: the body is my friend. In this relationship, the most powerful dimensions in life, our physical powers and our intellectual and spiritual energies mutually seek nearness and completion in each other rather than supremacy or hostility. A healthy mind in a healthy, well-disciplined body becomes the norm.

The definition of man as an animal endowed with reason concedes the existence in his nature of two elements, a material and a spiritual entity. Each will flourish best when supported by the other, and the more we succeed in creating a synthesis between the two, the greater is the accord between the diverse forces.

The harmonious coexistence of mind and body does not exclude a position of priority. Physical appetites and spiritual dictates may collide, and when they do, the final word must come from balanced reason. "Let

---

* Sri Isopanisad, introduced and translated by A. C. Bhaktivedanta Swami Prabhupada (Los Angeles: The Bhaktivedanta Book Trust, 1969), p. 50, rule 12.

me put it like this: if you are guided by the Spirit you will be in no danger of yielding to self-indulgence, since self-indulgence is the opposite of the Spirit, the Spirit is totally against such a thing, and it is precisely because the two are so opposed that you do not always carry out your good intentions. If you are led by the Spirit, no law can touch you" (Ga 5:16–18).

When our body is a friend, we have to grant it care and privileges which condition our well-being. If, in youth, we abuse its resources, enjoying a fast life for its own sake, we jeopardize our future growth and condemn ourselves to an old age plagued with regrets. God's design has established a particular rhythm in our body which has a language of its own. It is our responsibility to understand its signals and be alert to its warnings.

Interference with this well-ordered plan of nature and a disregard of its inner alarms has become a popular habit in our time, followed without consideration of the consequences. Our restless generation is impatient with time and obsessed with the *now*. The art of waiting, of giving nature the time it needs to grow and heal, has been replaced with a now-or-never philosophy. Instant action is demanded, and if nature refuses to oblige, chemicals will.

Our nervous system today is burdened with demands unknown in the past. One crisis following another strains our mental, emotional, and physical powers to such an extent that we seldom find the peace and total relaxation which our body needs to function at its best. Emotional upsets produce physical stress and our mental woes and worries are translated from the language of the mind to the sensations of the body. The heart beats faster, blood pressure rises, our glands work overtime when trouble besieges the self. Yet if there are no burdens at all and no crises, the suffering may be no less, for boredom, innocent as it may appear, alienates us from life, sucking at our vital energies and disturbing a healthy balance between challenge and response.

If order is nature's law, then order must become the law by which we regulate our body's share of work and rest, activity and leisure. Occasional stress can easily be absorbed, but if allowed to continue too long it undermines our defense systems. Whether the tensions result from our own overindulgence or from our inability to cope with the frustrations in our life makes little difference. Each of us, by our own inner discipline and our own physical and spiritual capacity, must work out an effective way to release our tensions and defuse the causes of our stress. What may be too little for one can be too much for another. The exuberance which one should restrain may be precisely what the other needs to spring to life.

Many of our pressures can be avoided. It is we ourselves who have accelerated the speed of our life, and we ourselves can slow it down. Either we make ourselves slaves to time by letting haste decide our course, or we master time by shaping it to our needs. Discipline—a rather ominous word in our permissive society—can clearly indicate what should be curtailed so that spiritual values can be planted in its place and grow in our souls.

Once we convince ourselves that not all bodily activities are commendable and innocent, we should be able to take the second step and say No to some of the demands of our appetites and some of the urgings of our passions. Given only one body which must last a lifetime, we have to be cautious in our treatment of this special friend. Though it is without doubt often tough, resilient, adaptable, able to bear excessive strains and to survive even our foolishness, we have no right to jeopardize its resources to the point of exhaustion if moderate and disciplined measures will suffice. If we cannot be the star of all attractions, let us be content to play a lesser role sometimes, or even on occasion, to withdraw from the cast altogether.

An honest self-examination may reveal that part of our stress comes from our efforts to cover up our shortcomings and failures, which are probably well known anyway. Perhaps humility and a sense of humor would allow us cheerfully to admit that we are not perfect and have not achieved all that we have dreamed about. Pretense takes a terrible toll, and those who seek its fragile shelter are to be pitied. They are the ones who swallow their own poison. "Arrogance, what advantage has this brought us? Wealth and boasting, what have these conferred on us? All those things have passed like a shadow, passed like a fleeting rumour. Like a ship that cuts through heaving waves—leaving no trace to show where it has passed" (Ws 5:8–10).

Medical science has gained in our day impressive insights into the functions of particular organs, and for these scientific accomplishments we are deeply grateful. But let us never lose a meaningful contact with our body as a whole by being absorbed with the health of its particular parts. Even trained specialists are apt to lose sight of the intimate interplay of the totality of bodily forces while focusing only on their particular field, sometimes with disastrous effects for the patient. Machines can be taken apart and dissected but not the pride of God's creation, the human body. "Instead of that, God put all the separate parts into the body on purpose. If all the parts were the same, how could it be a body? As it is, the parts are many but the body is one" (I Co 12:18–19).

Our body has to be accepted in its wholeness. The wide range of its forces and energies must be respected, sexuality included. Sex, long considered a tasteless word better left unspoken, has emerged from the tumult of our times as a tremendous force to be reckoned with, not only in one's own body but in our civilization as a whole. Our outlook on life, our ideals, the way we question the purpose and ends of our existence, are all influenced at least to some degree by our attitude toward our sexual powers. We can suppress the energies of sexual life, but to deny its influence is futile.

Sexuality and spirituality were never meant to be separated by mutually excluding walls. It was God's design to coordinate the redeeming features of the two in a fruitful harmony. Sexuality without spirituality can easily lead to an incontinent promiscuity that destroys all awareness of man's higher destiny, while spirituality without a healthy awareness of sexuality can develop into an arid inhumanity that drains from our hearts all tenderness and warmth. To achieve an honest and livable balance between these two tremendous forces is not the easiest task that faces humanity's never-resting search for dignity and freedom.

Sexual desires, which can be boundless, should

never be equated with sexual needs. Our modern civilization—if it deserves that name—stimulates these desires in its people without any care for age or mentality. Day and night the sexual instincts are provoked by films, shoddy publications, and business, even by so-called cultural programs, as if all expectations and aspirations of man were fulfilled by sexual satisfactions. The moral confusions, the ever-increasing cases of mental and psychic disorders, the crime rate which spirals beyond control, are only a few of the danger signals warning us that we have chosen a road that can end in disaster.

To follow the whims of our appetites as slaves follow a master's call, might bring some momentary relaxation but never the inner harmony which our mind seeks with our body. Obsessive sex annihilates the road to unification and leaves a person alone with his guilt and self-hatred. "Do not follow your lusts, restrain your desires. If you allow yourself to satisfy your desires, this will make you the laughing stock of your enemies" (Si 18:30–31).

Sexual needs vary in individuals according to biological structure, personal convictions, and one's state in life. We ourselves, guided by mature insights, must decide in our own conscience how to cope with them. The belief that in order to become fully human one must gratify all one's sexual desires has been disproved over and again by both historical reality and medical data.

In any final solution—if a final solution ever can be found—mind and body must assert and be granted their separate rights and fulfill their separate functions. Together they can form a masterpiece; separated from each other's influence, they might bring forth a suffering being, distorted and unbalanced. "In my inmost self I dearly love God's Law, but I can see that my body follows a different law that battles against the law which my reason dictates. This is what makes me a prisoner of that law of sin which lives inside my body" (Rm 7:22–23).

Often a crisis is what brings mind and body from a state of precarious ambivalence to a tested permanence. Cleansed by sufferings, the spiritual and bodily forces deepen their appreciation of each other and extend healing and a merciful justice to each other's rights and needs.

This healing has the beginning and end in thought. The moment our way of thinking enters a more spiritual plane, our physical powers improve. In the same proportion as our ideas are purified, salutary effects on our body ensue. If God had no difficulty in cleansing a leper, he can surely cure a distraught mind and body.

There is a wide area in life where no *Must* signs are posted; our characters are challenged to do things not required of us, to obey where there is no obligation forcing us, and to give when no one demands a gift. It is especially in this area that the authenticity of our character is judged. As we act in these unforeseen situations, without time to pretend, we reveal ourselves as we really are. The strength of our inner courage measures the worth of our character, which is something far greater than any material riches the world can offer. Even a beggar stripped of possessions and influence can count these riches.

Our body, a cherished friend for all the years of our life, will never regret its faithful dedication. When its generous service is finally terminated by death, this trustworthy servant will not be discarded and forgotten but will be rewarded as a friend should be. "For us, our homeland is in heaven, and from heaven comes the saviour we are waiting for, the Lord Jesus Christ, and he will transfigure these wretched bodies of ours into copies of his glorious body. He will do that by the same power with which he can subdue the whole universe" (Ph 3:20–21).

And so, this body of ours, which began its long journey on a troubled earth will at last find fulfillment. The unfinished mystery, kept hidden and restrained all the days of our life, will now confront the *Mysterium tremendum:* God, who created heaven and earth and all things that are in the universe, and who will judge what we have done with our body—whether it has been our Master, our Enemy, or our Friend.

chapter 9

YOUNG AND OLD . . . . .

sunrise/sunset

I am the child of sunrise,
Of wonder, power and might;
Too soon, at sunset, I become
An old man of the light.

THE CHILD IN ME

Life preserves a rhythm, diverse in many aspects, yet similar in its permanent undercurrent. Days following each other vary in individual expressions but remain the same in essential structure.

Like nature, life adjusts well to the elements of variety while it takes the laws of constancy for granted. Whether a day is filled with excitement or boring in its emptiness, noon is followed by evening and the night is redeemed by the sun of the new day.

Man too, so different in personal characteristics, comes to the realization that what awakens first in all of us is the child. In the beginning we are young, old age follows later. Only a few are born old.

Christ, when asked to explain the essence of humanity, answered simply, "Be like this child."

What did he mean by this divine command? What kind of obligation arises from such an unexpected order? What makes a child so attractive in the eyes of the divine? Do we *still* possess this childlike quality in our soul or have we, long ago, lost its preciousness in our hearts?

The child is forever growing into what is yet to be. Not only do the bodily dimensions change but, and much more, the mental capacities, which grow in depth and understanding. Many are the transformations that take place in the life of a child in the short span of a year. "How different you look since last I saw you," we say, when taken by surprise at a youngster's unexpected growth.

Children do not know what to do with limitations. Seldom content with what they have, their youthful drive opens doors which others are afraid to touch. Cautions are calmly refused if they cool down the fever of enthusiasm, while boundaries are defied if they destroy the passion for a better life.

With less of wisdom and more of courage, children pursue relentlessly the goal they have in mind. Thoughts of rest cannot tempt them until they have achieved what they believe is destiny. To surrender or give up is as out of the question as any compromise with second best. All or nothing is the only sign on their horizon, and in between these two extremes little else exists.

The child's inner growth is firmly rooted in personal feelings. Others' experiences rarely count because they convey a message that the child cannot integrate in his own imagination. Events are judged in a light that is pure and absolute. Practical considerations and political realities have not yet become standards by which the young measure the value of deeds.

Children say what they mean: double talk has not yet falsified their tongues. With more honesty than diplomacy they report life as they see it; no other considerations influence their rendition of happenings. Even in those precarious moments when the listener would prefer to hear a lie, the child retorts, "So it happened."

The young harbor no suspicions. They believe what they hear and praise what they see. Invitations are accepted without any thought of which are good and which are not. "Anyone who welcomes a little child like this in my name welcomes me. But anyone who is an obstacle to bring down one of these little ones who have faith in me would be better drowned in the depths of the sea with a great millstone round his neck" (Mt 18:5–6).

Real innocence has to be considered a quality of heart which only the child possesses in its fullness. The outer world and the inner heaven are one glorious land in which the youngster is the undisputed ruler. Heart and mind are so strongly united that no promises or threats can easily alter their course. They are not concerned with class lines which adults draw into life to separate human beings according to creed, race, and color.

Even when children try to deceive, the attempt is so clumsy that before deception takes place, truth blushes on their cheeks. Not quite experienced in the art of betrayal, they cannot hide their motives or camouflage the truth. It is typical of some adults to serve two masters. They can agree with one without disagreeing with the other, thus concealing their real intention. Perhaps it is too strong to assert that "man is what he hides" but it is more than likely that nearly everyone has at some time been deceptive.

Innocence graces the act of giving and the art of receiving. The child's gift is offered for the pure joy of giving without considering the possibilities of a pleasant return. The excitement and joy in the other's eyes is enough for the child. Friends and strangers alike feel the warmth of such a gift and both are treated with equal consideration.

The things which catch a child's attention may be small in themselves but are great in the eyes of the young. The full power of their emotions are invested and the event assumes a stature as wide as the world.

Watching eagerly for the slightest sign of recognition, the child demands attention even if we have no intention of giving it. The attention which love provides is greedily devoured by the child who never thinks he has enough. We express the child in us whenever we say to another, "I love you dearly."

Children do not know how to hate. It could be that hate is not an inborn trait of human nature but a quality acquired later in life. It creates distance, eliminates nearness between human beings. Adults in conflict with each other avoid contact, while the child, offended or not, returns to friend or foe. "Let the little children alone, and do not stop them coming to me; for it is to such as these that the kingdom of heaven belongs" (Mt 19:14–15).

With an almost mythical faith, children believe in the impossible. Life, which presents itself to their imagination in tiny episodes, never in its full view, is seen less of a problem than it really is. Need we confess that sometimes we pity children and wish they would grow up so that they will learn more quickly to be what they are not?

A world destroyed is inconceivable to the young

mind since life, like the dream, must go on forever. How disturbed a child can become when death is met for the first time!

Imaginary gains can be as real to a child as real losses are imaginary. Somehow he is always on the winning side since he does not know how to lose. With tears or laughter, he salvages ruins and calls them castles, and of bits of wreckage he makes the greatest ship that ever sailed the sea.

Although, to an adult, prayer is often an artificial gesture, it is as natural as singing and laughing to the child. Heaven, which for us may be a problem to be solved, provides the child with a home away from home. To enjoy happiness in the world of angels is as instinctive to the young as to enjoy a happy hour with brothers and sisters. The heavenly father is just as near as the father on earth who shows love and comforts him. "I tell you solemnly, unless you change and become like little children you will never enter the kingdom of heaven. And so, the one who makes himself as little as this little child is the greatest in the kingdom of heaven" (Mt 18:3–4).

Have we betrayed the innocence of the child within us? Has simplicity and honesty been discarded like things which have lost their use? Have we changed the child in us into an image unworthy of description?

Why are we ill at ease with innocence? Instead of fostering it, why are we so eager to outgrow its effects on our thinking? To be called "innocent" is taken more as a reproach than praise. Yet innocence, as a quality of mind, is creative. Poets and artists rely on its inspiration to write about life as it is, or dream about life as it should be. Paintings, novels, immortal poems are not only the work of disciplined minds put into action but also the effects of the genius of man inspired by a vision of innocence and purity. There is no greater power than the one which is sparked when divine innocence meets the innocence of a person's soul. It was just such an encounter that brought us Francis of Assisi.

Saints and artists are not far apart; both have a message needed by mankind to keep faith alive. One expresses with his life a divine mystery while the other expresses with his hand the reflection of that mystery in the world.

Contrarily, however, the innocence which does not affect one's thinking but relates only to the world of emotions can stem the tide of creativity. To feel that the events in life must end happily as a fairytale is an insult to our intelligence, but it is much more damaging to delude with such fantasies the ones who look to us for guidance. Childish behavior is a dubious asset for anyone in a responsible position.

Emotional innocence or uninformed naïveté is blind to the raw material of life. To see only goodness on all sides, without realizing the possible evil, is to excuse ourselves from the duty of finding ways to correct the evil and promote all that is good. "Remember, I am sending you out like sheep among wolves; so be cunning as serpents and yet as harmless as doves" (Mt 10:16).

Innocence can bring elements of contradiction into our decisions. Our natural instinct to avoid being sacrificed or misled by others who are shrewd in their tactics of survival is so powerful that innocence is often brushed aside in favor of aggression. "An eye for an eye," which balances one evil with another, seems for some the best way to repay an insult. Revenge first and innocence later is the practical logic of an aggressor.

The strategy of revenge will never inspire a lasting solution in a crisis. Convincing as it may seem to the hearts of the realists, it only deepens a conflict to the point of no return. If innocence is gone, can chaos be far behind?

What's Old In Me?

No matter how hard we try to keep the child in us alive, we cannot stop the curious process of aging. We may have succeeded in capturing the fountain of youth in spirit, but we still find our hair turns grey, our eyes grow dim, and the machinery of our body wears out. Cherished memories, with all their colorful details and happy endings, lose their charm; all that is retained from years gone by can be expressed in the one enigmatic sentence, "Didn't we meet years ago?"

Attention to the never-ending flow of new events makes us incapable of sustained concentration. If asked to describe a meeting with friends, we falter and make excuses that it is easy to forget. Oblivious to the excitement which stirs the curiosity of others, we gradually narrow our sphere of life to the things which now seem essential. We fall into a sort of primitive state as our body begins to express, in bleak and pathetic language, how vulnerable we are to the merciless dictates of time. Our decisions are made with less originality. Old ideas are treasured while new ones actually bring pain instead of exaltation. We prefer that the world stand still at least as long as we are on it—that the restless thoughts stay at a distance, like the stranger we don't care to see.

Progress is pure nuisance; it disturbs a past that was the most beautiful of all times. For old age, the best change seems to be no change at all. Friends of years gone by become more precious and appreciated since we are accustomed to their faces and ways. Besides, new friends seem unreliable and seldom knock at our door. Without much of a choice, we hold on to what we have. Our passions, formerly all-consuming, gradually cool down and play a less aggressive part in the decisions of our life. Instead of love and hate, we finally offer understanding and compassion. Not that the fire ever dies, but the raging fury seems to be replaced by quietly glowing embers. Summer mellows into autumn, and autumn into winter, gentleness replaces revenge, war gives way to peace. "How fine a thing: sound judgment with grey hairs, and for greybeards to know how to advise! How fine a thing: wisdom in the aged, and considered advice coming from men of distinction! The crown of old men is ripe experience, their true glory, the fear of the Lord" (Si 25:4–6).

Nature has a mysterious ability to compensate. What old age loses physically, it gains in wisdom. Emotional thrills gradually become less rewarding while inner peace of mind intensifies until it reaches a depth of understanding never before sensed. In many ways, our later years remind us of the setting sun. Is there any spectacle greater than the splendor of the sun before it sets? The dying ball of fire reserves its most impressive grandeur for its parting bow to earth when it sets aflame all corners of a silent heaven. Are not some aspects of old age comparable to the beauty of this moving scene? Both seem to prefer to offer the greatest prize at the closing moments.

The very eyes of those who enjoy their closing years radiate a peace which reminds us more of heaven than of earth, and as we listen to their words, we feel their deep insights and understanding. Haven't we all enjoyed the company of some serene older folks whose outer beauty has worn thin only to let the inner tenderness break through and reign supreme? "Now that I am old and grey, God, do not desert me; let me live to tell the rising generation about your strength and power, about your heavenly righteousness, God" (Ps 71:18–19).

Of course not all of our elderly impress us so favorably. Some let the outer beauty fade away and neglect to fill in the void with other values. Far from becoming calm and serene, they strengthen their demands and complaints. Rather than stepping back to give the younger generation a chance, they become more domineering and presuming than ever. They grow touchy about their privileges and cling to their possessions with a stubbornness and greed that forbids any thoughts that their way on earth will ever come to an end.

One group grows old gently, the other ages harshly. The difference between the two is their preparation.

When the retiring years appear, a gradual slowdown of the hectic schedule with increasingly long intervals of leisure works for a healthy transition. Abrupt endings seldom have a healing effect. To work feverishly until the moment old age stops the clock of labor is the worst way to prepare for the arrival of the inevitable event of leisure.

Talents and hobbies developed long before the time of retirement will absorb our interest when other interests have flown and friends begin to abandon our ship. To retire into nothing but a vague emptiness is too boresome a burden to endure. Man, born to work, to think, to create, must remain alive until he dies. "If you have gathered nothing in your youth, how can you find anything in your old age?" (Si 25:3).

Old age surely does not sail in like a dreamboat, nor does it crash the gate like an intruder. It is neither enemy territory luring us to defeat nor the fringe of paradise offering invitation to pleasure. It is only life continued on a more modest scale, with ambitions and desires realistically adjusted.

Unlike any other civilization, ours seems unable to solve the problems created by old age. How quickly we become impatient with the old and their pattern of senility, forgetting that very soon we ourselves will be in the same condition! How often we hide them in cages, golden on the outside but depressing on the inside so that their presence will not remind us what we owe them! Their expenses, if we pay them, seem to absolve us of further responsibilities. We forget rather easily that *expenses paid* never quite equals *love spent*. "Do not reject me now I am old, nor desert me now my strength is failing, for my enemies are uttering threats, spies hatching their conspiracy" (Ps 71:9–10).

A high degree of sensitivity is needed to identify with the inner world of people who are aged and alone. To feel the message of their loneliness, to sense their hunger for companionship is a privilege for those who freely admit their own desire for friends and the pressing need to share and communicate.

The needs of the old are, after all, the same as the needs of the young. If they would become more conscious of the sameness of their expectations, they would not flee each other's presence but would seek each other's company. Were more of the elderly willing to share with the young the priceless qualities of maturity, old age would be less of a problem and more of a blessing, enriching both those who need and those who give.

Old and *young* exist in the same person. We like an old friend for what is young in him and are attracted to the young who show a wisdom which graces the old. Those who group people by their age or level of interest benefit few, while the perceptive ones who unite the various aspirations are a blessing to humanity. "My son, support your father in his old age, do not grieve him during his life. Even if his mind should fail, show him sympathy, do not despise him in your health and strength; for kindness to a father shall not be forgotten but will serve as a reparation for your sins" (Si 3:12–14).

To see only the sunny side of life is unreal while to portray only its darkness is unfair. More than ever the youth of today need to be reassured of the beauty hidden in life. Modern art, literature, novels, films, television, and newspapers all project with savage monotony the underworld of life, glamorizing evil and belittling what is good in man.

Our youngsters have grown up in an environment without innocence and have been led to believe that life is nothing but money, sex, and death. Why try to be honest if dishonesty is the practical way of life? Why be responsible and pure in an age of frivolity and crime?

Old age, with life already fully experienced and viewed with all its glories and defeats, can restore again the balance on the scales of human destiny. The old one, advanced in years and wisdom, is best suited to pierce the shadows and concentrate on the radiant. The fear of the ever-present liabilities of life has been replaced with the freedom to have faith in the goodness and trust of humanity. To believe first and always in the honesty of man while not overlooking his capacities for evil is a sign of true balance. "You have done great things; who, God, is comparable to you? You have sent me misery and hardship, but you will give me life again, you will pull me up again from the depths of the earth, prolong my old age, and once more comfort me" (Ps 71:19–20).

If there is still a quality of life which should challenge the aged, it is forgiveness. Having accomplished what they expected with the mysteries of life, those who have grown old with grace are finally in a position to live with the imperfections of others. Strong and faithful in their feelings, they can easily put up with the disagreements they meet in life. Contradictions or offenses disturb them little since they remember clearly their own failings. Instead of complaining, "How do you dare?" they answer reassuringly "We understand, we forgive."

What are the thoughts of people approaching the evening hours of life? What do they remember when their life parades for its last show? What are their reflections when diaries are opened and reread?

For many, it seems that life has passed too quickly. How strange it all has been! Was it a dream or was it real? How could it happen the way it did, and why were we chosen for the particular part we played?

Would we do it all over again, or would we take a different direction?

What counts in life finally becomes real to us, while the things which once bothered us are relegated to oblivion. The highlights of our life take on new importance, while the petty things are discarded without regret.

There is a strong desire to tidy up and put loose ends together. Everything should be in order so that whenever the hour of departure arrives, we are ready. Gains and losses are relived, and we see that what we considered a loss was, in the final count, really a gain. How poor a story it would make if we had allowed our disappointments to overrule our youthful hopes!

Not much will change until the evening turns to night. There will be periods of loneliness, some happy moments with loved ones, and, in spite of all the failures that have darkened our past, a deep persistent hope for the better life to come. Reconciled with defeat and success the old man in us will be able to bear them both in peace.

For, after all, life has been good to us. It reflected the meaning we imposed on it. We have no reason for sorrow, no cause to complain, it was life fully lived. And now we must wait to be judged by a God who was human in everything except sin.

chapter 10

THE OTHER . . . . .

the star

Mine eyes have set upon the star
I beg that I may follow,
To find the path of truth; that I
Be worthy of tomorrow.

OUR LOVE FOR THE OTHER

In his short career on earth, Christ was not interested in the big move toward worldly power. The dramatic play for self-glory never caught his attention. Earthly might expressed in impressive numbers and massive influence was totally left out in the divine strategy, not because it was evil in itself, but because it was useless.

The new message Christ came to announce was radically different from all the power plays of the past. His demands, unheard of in human history, stressed ideals which proved not only unpopular with the Israelites but also hard on human nature. The powerful were replaced by the meek and humble while kings and princes were asked to become more like the innocent children. The unknown triumphed over the known.

117

The self was not important in the hierarchy of values, but the *other*. What would be done for others would be of greater interest to the Lord than all the treasures collected for personal satisfaction.

The gifts we carefully take for ourselves become meaningless in God's accounting, while gifts laid at the door of others stir the approval of eternal love. What we enjoy alone creates but little pleasure; what we share with others becomes twice as meaningful. A journey made alone remains alone, while traveling together writes a book of happy memories. Only what we have given away will ever be really ours; what we divide on earth will be multiplied in heaven.

Who is the *other?* Who is this mysterious person described in Holy Scripture as our neighbor? Is he the brother we grew up with, the friend at school, the stranger on the bus? Could he be my enemy?

Our Lord never dictated a list of names which would indicate those who deserve our special attention and affection. No *Who's Who* naming those who have a priority on our heart has ever been published. If our Lord had clearly selected a certain group of people worthy of our affection, wouldn't he have excluded another group equally in need of our devotion? Wouldn't we have interpreted the command to love *this person* as permission to ignore *that person?*

Barriers have never been favored in God's mind. Anything that creates division is abhorred. "Be united amongst yourselves" was his holy wish, not only for his scattered apostles, but for all who would follow in his footsteps.

Have we any clue to help us in the difficult job of choosing our friends? Is there a criterion we can apply to find a solution? After all, no one can love the whole world, and those who claim they do might love only themselves.

Who, then, is this person we must invite into our homes, show our love to and care for? Who has a claim on our time, our attention, and our daily bread? Whom must we help when help is needed?

Perhaps God would say it is the man who has no one but us. If we are the only ones who can open the door which others have shut, we must open it. If we are the only ones to hear the plea for assistance, we must rush to his side. If we are the only ones able to lessen his pain, and we refuse, we are guilty of a sin which may not easily be forgiven. If we are the only ones to possess the light, we cannot use it to brighten only our path. The man who has no one but us is sent our way by God. He is the one who becomes a brother, a neighbor, a friend. We have to stop and find out what causes his pain; we have to listen to him and share his troubles and anxieties.

What we like or dislike is not of primary importance in the divine economy. The overriding issue is the person in need. What is planned for our pleasure must be delayed for the sake of what must be done for the other. Our actual presence is needed, not long distance calls, and our actual help is desired more than just our good intentions. Even prayers, precious as they always are, must be accompanied by deeds. "I tell you solemnly, in so far as you neglected to do this to one of the least of these, you neglected to do it to me" (Mt 25:45).

Not everyone can become our friend, but everybody must be treated as an individual. The God-given rights of others impose on all of us duties which we cannot bypass without scarring our conscience. To

treat another merely as a shadow to our sun is forgetting that in the sight of God, the other is as precious as
we can ever be.

When we classify others as worthy and unworthy, or
equal and not-so-equal, we may be using human terms
to foster or protect our own special interests. Our
thought about what is good for us veers away from
divine concern of what is good for others, and the
values we choose infringe on the stern commands of
God.

The more we sever relationships, the more we
deepen the roots of mutual distrust, and separation ensues. But separation is a man-made solution, while
unity is what the divine heart requests.

Self-love, camouflaged as concern for others, is a
common temptation which many of us have endured
and few have confessed. Often we single out a person
to shower with our affections, not because that person
is in need but because our own emotions crave an
outlet. The "I like you" is often a substitute for the "I
need you," while "I dislike you" stands for "You are of
no help to me." To let our personal feelings become
the only measure for inviting or refusing relationships
is cruel and selfish. "My son, do not refuse the poor a
livelihood, do not tantalise the needy. Do not add to
the sufferings of the hungry, do not bait a man in distress. Do not aggravate a heart already angry, nor keep
the destitute waiting for your alms. Do not repulse a
hard-pressed beggar, nor turn your face from a poor
man" (Si 4:1–4).

No one will ever fall so low that we cannot discover
something in his personality that is worthy of recognition. Every member of our human family, the social
derelict included, reveals in the deepest ground of his

being a certain quality that merits imitation. It is up to our sensitivities of faith to unveil that good and acknowledge it. No one on earth is obliged to prove to us his worth; it is up to us to discover it.

When the human frailties of others disappoint us, it only shows that we still set our own conditions on whom to love and how. A conditioned love is a poor imitation of real love which gives of itself without asking anything in return. "You have learnt how it was said: You must love your neighbour and hate your enemy. But I say this to you: love your enemies and pray for those who persecute you; in this way you will be sons of your Father in heaven, for he causes his sun to rise on bad men as well as good, and his rain to fall on honest and dishonest men alike. For if you love those who love you, what right have you to claim any credit?" (Mt 5:43–47).

Dislike can also be caused by lack of understanding. We met the other on the surface, and on the surface our relationship remained. Had we given more attention to studying the other's temperament, we would have found solutions to puzzles which otherwise remain unsolved. Had we looked deeper and tried harder to hear what the other did not say, we might have perceived an entirely different person. To avoid a person we dislike is the primitive reaction; to get to know this person better is the response graced by God. Not only are we our brother's keeper; we are also our brother's maker.

Compassion, perhaps more than anything else, should let us see the good in others and the evil in ourselves. The more conscious we are of our own hideouts, the more generous we are in allowing excuses to others, since an unbiased self-knowledge readily grants respect and honor to all. Only the proverbial heart of stone will drive a hard bargain with one who is down and out.

One should never identify a person by an obvious weakness. To think of someone as a liar or a thief because he was once guilty of lying or stealing proves that we know little about human frailties and strengths. The motivations for actions performed in anger or in shame are often so intricate that even the liar or thief is at a loss to explain his reasoning. To steal for love or for hunger is far different from malicious theft, just as lying to defend a friend is less disgraceful than the lie which hides personal guilt.

When we say to another, "You should not have done that" without inquiring into the *why* of his deed, we indicate how little we know of ourselves. So often it is the grace of God alone that keeps us clear of actions which would later bring us to shame also.

We should be slow in taking the final step of giving up on others. To say it is too late for rescue can be more of an escape than the truth, for if rescue calls for sacrifice, we may be eager to let the curtain fall. Besides, can we ever be sure that the other is really lost? Aren't we infringing on the domain of the divine? If our Lord refuses to declare a person hopeless, why should we assume the right to pronounce such a verdict? Until the last hour of life, each of us should live in the hope that our best will triumph in the end. "I became more wretched and Thou more close to me. Thy right hand was ready to pluck me from the mire and wash me clean, though I knew it not."*

* *The Confessions of St. Augustine,* translated by F. J. Sheed (New York: Sheed & Ward, 1943), VI: 16.

Do we ever see ourselves as we really are? To be unbiased about our own person is a "possible impossibility"; we need others to point out the truth, to tell us how unpleasant we can be.

It is not by accident but by divine design that we are social beings who can mature and understand ourselves through a continuing dialogue with others. Yet we know that sometimes this ideal conversation fails to take place. At the most critical times, when we cry out for help, we find that no one wants to hear what we are going through, and we have to carry a great burden alone. Much of our important learning will be done completely on our own, without any help.

We suffer to the degree that we fail to build a bridge into the mystery of the other. Living in a world of lonely streets where no one walks except ourselves is as destructive to our minds as it is debilitating to our souls. It may cause harsh moments in our life when our gifts find no receiver, but how bitter the experience if we refuse to share what is ours. And yet, these painful moments could have been avoided if we had pierced the veil of darkness with the light of understanding and friendship.

The measure of one's happiness or unhappiness on earth is largely the success or failure in human relationships. Whoever is cynical enough to presume that the other is the stepping-stone to hell may be already creating his own hell on earth. But if our emotions and ideas blend with those we meet, inner peace becomes second nature, and we share in its blessing.

Among those we deal with in our daily world, we find some who are born for themselves. Their own ego takes precedence over all other voices. Reserved and cold, they take a long time to issue invitations. They opt for love at a distance which provides the sanctuary they need to overcome suspicions and distrust. On the surface they appear remote, but in their hearts they hide affections which are released with difficulty and restraint. If at last they begin to trust, their obligations are assumed and well-fulfilled. A hesitant beginning can find a blessed end. Occasionally we come across people who impress us at first sight with a carefree disregard of their own necessities; they are the ones born for others. It is natural for them to be friendly, to enter into relationships and share what they have. Gladly they walk the extra mile the other cannot walk alone. Theirs is a gift from heaven, a charisma richly lived for others. How lucky we are when we have such a friend.

Whether love comes on wings or in chains, it must survive and prosper. Without it, you and I cannot make it through life. No power on earth can keep us from opening our hearts as a shelter for others. For all of us, God has commanded: *Love each other as you love yourselves.*

The other expects to be accepted on his own terms, not as we wish him to be. Each of us offers an individuality which is unrepeatable in intensity and unique in its fashion. Each one reflects a particular glory and has a special reason to exist. The song of joy which our life sings is written for our voice alone; no one else can hum its tune.

We are all at our best when we like what we love and at our worst when we dislike what we should love. It takes character to remain faithful to a dream after it is broken. To love when the other becomes unlovable

is a rare achievement. Today, in ever-growing num-
bers, people joined by vows made in the presence of
God abandon each other for the most trivial reasons.
That their children suffer seems totally irrelevant.
Self-survival seems to be all that matters.

Love, once considered holy, has turned into a dubious exchange of sexual favors. Promises to remain
faithful until death have been cheapened by empty
rhetoric, announced without conviction and received
without faith. A sacred marriage is considered a relic
of the past which few desire to imitate.

Have vows lost their right to be made? Have promises turned into nightmares? Has the Yes we gave to
another moved only our lips without touching the core
of our being? How long can a civilization last in which
its greatest asset—love—has been betrayed? If faith in
promises disappears, what else is left for future generations?

Fewer people than we might suppose really act
maliciously, but they do exist. Suspicious that the
other harbors evil with intent to destroy, they move to
strike first. Not everything that seems malicious stems
from malice, however. Other motivations can grow in
our hearts which lead us to destroy the bond with
others. Inner sufferings, failures, and loneliness can
weaken a vow so much that it flutters helplessly, like a
leaf in the autumn gale. Revenge held too long breaks
loose and overshadows the memories of better years.
Physical or emotional exhaustion can enervate the will
to love to such a degree that any additional burden
imposed by others becomes unbearable. "Father forgive them for they do not know what they are doing."

Love, then, is a positive action, not a studied definition. Its center is in doing, not in feeling. Distant promises cannot equal a needed presence and letters alone cannot substitute for the personal touch.

Love, which became for Christ the ultimate, has to be expressed in deeds. What we have actually done for others, not what we wished to do, will be remembered on the day of reckoning. To preach and teach Christ is one thing; to meet him in our love for others is something else. Real faith, based on courage, ties the profession of faith into the often cruel demands of life. A most recent testimony of "faith tested" was rendered to us by a man who refused to live for himself when a chance was offered to die for another.

It began in the grim setting of an infamous concentration camp. Terror paralyzed the nearly lifeless bodies of the prisoners as word spread through the cells that ten men would pay with their lives for one man who had escaped. Among those chosen to die, one cried in desperation. "Oh my poor wife, my poor children, I shall never see them again!" Was he crying in vain? Did his voice become lost in the despair of human wilderness without being heard? Was he really expecting a fellow prisoner already branded by the torment of human hell to take his place in the march of death?

Suddenly a slight figure stepped forward to face the arrogant and domineering commander. "I would like to die in place of one of the men you have condemned." Whether from astonished disbelief or stunned curiosity, the cruel executioner allowed the heroic exchange to take place. Fr. Maximilian Kolbe, the Franciscan priest from Poland who in his youth had vowed himself to Mary, was led to the starvation bunker where he died in dignity and freedom.

Was this exchange of lives purely the childish act of an ignorant religious? Was he throwing his life away because he didn't know what else to do with it?

Father Kolbe knew what he was doing. This choice was not only inspired by his intellect alone, but by a superior motivation far beyond any intellectual conclusion. When he saw his neighbor in peril, his own self was forgotten. Not the safety of his own security dominated his thinking, but the fate of the other who was in danger.

What would our reactions have been? Would we hide behind others or perhaps profess a sympathy expressed in words alone? How strong is our dedication and love for others? Can we bear, at least, part of their cross? Or, are we all breathing a sigh of relief when we are not put to the test? Isn't our faith much stronger in words than it is in deeds?

Whatever we give to others, be it our life, our love, or our treasures, let us give it with the deep conviction that the other whom we can see is the vestige of a God we cannot see. Love made visible in others is the only love worthy of its name.

God's Love for Us

How many misunderstandings and tensions are born of the indisputable fact that God's taste and our taste are so different. What we like, he often dislikes; for what we have preference, he has no use. Will we ever find a common base of action, or of judgment? Will we ever agree on anything?

Christ clearly champions the rights of the forgotten ones, the oppressed, those who never received their just due. For the short-changed ones, the by-passed, who never had enough of anything, he reserves the best seats around the altar, and assures them that they are very much remembered in the kingdom of heaven.

For I was hungry and you gave me food; I was thirsty and you gave me drink; I was a stranger and you made me welcome; naked and you clothed me, sick and you visited me, in prison and you came to see me" (Mt 25:35–37).

For I was hungry and you gave me food. Christ spoke first of the hungry. During all his life he was concerned about them. Man and hunger have always been partners, not by choice but by dire necessity. We never have enough, we always are in want of more; more food, money, power, influence, love—more of everything we can imagine. Are we ever really satisfied? Have we ever said to God, "Don't give it to me; give it to those who need it more?"

Physical hunger is a frightful reality felt the world around. That widespread starvation is the terrible fate of people in one corner of our globe while the other corner throws good food to the dogs is one of the heaviest burdens our modern conscience must bear. Nothing can excuse us from the serious obligation to remedy this situation to the best of our means. Hunger always shouts, making itself known in frightful slogans of revolutions or in pleading eyes that tear at our peace of mind. If Christians cannot heal the wounds of such injustice, others will. If we harden our hearts, the hungry ones might join forces and take from us what we refuse to give in love. A certain equality will be achieved one way or the other.

Whether the sounds of injustice disturb us depends on our character. If we react by fear alone, fear will capture our souls. If we are moved by love and compassion, faith will turn the wheels of history. When neither fear nor love can stimulate our action, then legal forces must bring forth justice.

Actually, we create more hunger than God ever intended to inflict on the world. Mismanagement and greed claim a longer list of casualties than natural catastrophes ever managed to compile. Man-made monsters destroy more lives than any earthquake ever claimed. The fast-rising rate of abandonment and abuse of children causes more suffering through lack of love than lack of proper nourishment.

What are the chances for a better world if our thinking is totally absorbed with the use of bombs that can obliterate not only our cities but mankind itself? The expenses of preparing for the modern means of total annihilation would surely provide a minimum of sustenance for all those who now perish by starvation. But what nation will change a budget of defense in favor of unselfish needs?

Our hearts hide another hunger which reaches far beyond our dinner table: hunger for God. Not by bread alone does man live, but by every word that leaves the mouth of God. We need God as much as we like to think he needs us. One without the other would be unthinkable. What body is without heart? This is man without faith: hollow and cold.

Hunger yearns to be stilled. The bread of earth is needed to fill the empty stomach and the bread of heaven is needed to ease the yearnings of the soul. Our revolutionary movements, social or political, which have aimed at alleviating the physical hunger alone, are now leading a perilous existence. Even if they ride the crest of popular favor for a little while, their real contributions to a better life are questionable. To solve the dilemma of injustice on purely materialistic terms replaces one hunger with another and greater one.

To focus on the social conditions of the twentieth century without taking into account the spiritual dimensions is asking each one of us to be content with being an animal and forget to be a man. "I am the bread of life. He who comes to me will never be hungry; he who believes in me will never thirst" (Jn 6:35).

I was thirsty and you gave me drink. It is difficult to know which is harder to endure, hunger or thirst. While hunger decimates the population, thirst robs the mind of its power. Three days without water and we cease to be human.

God gave us plenty of water; over seventy percent of the earth's surface is covered with oceans, lakes or rivers. In spite of this impressive surplus there are many plagued with thirst.

Bodily thirst, menacing as it is, presses hard on our lips, but it is little compared to the spiritual thirst that parches our soul and leads to despair. What can we really do if we are seared by the flame of guilt, drained by passions or fury of revenge? What can we say if we are alone with haunting memories of defeat or betrayal known only to ourselves?

Give me to drink refers just as much to understanding as to water. Relief is sought not only from refreshing fountains but from compassionate hearts. The assurance of a better day to come is needed by the man standing in the shadow of guilt, and such an assurance must be provided by us. Even a child can share glory; it takes a man to share shame. "If any man is thirsty, let him come to me! Let the man come and drink who believes in me! As scripture says: From his breast shall flow fountains of living water" (Jn 7:38).

I was a stranger and you made me welcome. We are all pilgrims on a journey without a beginning, on a trip that has no end. We arrive where we are not to stay but to move on; like different rivers flowing into the same ocean, different lives find the same destiny: the beyond.

Some strangers are right on course. They know the road well and walk it without fear. Theirs is a contented journey and they reach their destination without much help. Others lose their way. Off in different directions, they follow paths that peter out and lead nowhere. Without a goal in life they take any road as long as it is easy, and if their direction is questioned, they shrug their shoulders in confusion and go on.

In the cold of the night, we like nothing better than a warm shelter. "Please take me in, I have lost my way" are words we all have heard. How did we react to such a plea? Instinctively we feel ill at ease with the stranger. Fear of the unknown stirs resentments, unforseen demands upset our daily routine. Why did he have to come just now? Why at our door? Why can't he go on and leave us alone?

Man needs to pause and take rest. No one can go on forever. Those who seek relief in their journey may annoy us with their boldness or surprise us with their humility, but whatever their message, let us listen;

whatever their request, let us think before we say no. Behind the stranger might hide a friend.

Christ sensed the pain of the wanderer who cannot retrace his steps. The lost sheep received more attention than the ninety-nine safely in the fold. Why such a preference?

The safe ones can wait; their fate is not in jeopardy. Any later moment is a good one for them and any later return is still on time. But the errant sheep can lose life forever. There is so much at stake that only immediate action has a chance to ward off danger. A slight delay is apt to be fatal. There is no choice but immediate rescue.

The secret restlessness of man, the desire to be somewhere else than where we are, brings the stranger at the door nearer to the stranger in our heart. Discontent with our surroundings makes us yearn for the promised land where everything is exciting, everything is beautiful. Bored with our daily repetitions, we seek escape into worlds of phantasy and vision unmarked on our map of life. Wasn't it man who invented Shangri-la?

So, then, the stranger is not so strange after all. He follows through on the things we would have liked to do, and his courage revives memories we long ago allowed to fall asleep. Doesn't he give to us much more than we can ever give to him? "If a stranger lives with you in your land, do not molest him. You must count him as one of your own countrymen and love him as yourself—for you were once strangers yourselves in Egypt. I am Yahweh your God" (Lv 19:33–34).

I was naked and you clothed me. Nakedness is man's most natural lot in life. He had nothing when life was given and he will have nothing when life is taken. As God has made us, so shall we return at the moment of our last accounting.

Nudity, a parody of nakedness, becomes a highly favored form of entertainment in times of moral confusion. Tasteless shows and questionable magazines picture the undressed body as an object of obscenity. To stimulate tired senses, the masterpiece of God's creation is degraded to the level of amusement, unworthy to be staged and unfit to be viewed.

A naked soul is as defenseless as a body exposed. Both ask for protection as both crave seclusion. Whenever we reveal a secret involving the guilt of others, we open wounds long since healed. Indiscretions forgotten become interesting news when we are too weak for silence. Someone's shame appears in headlines since we insist on revenge. Our way of seeking justice damages another's reputation and we still feel we did right. Isn't it a frightful thought that one man will gain satisfaction by destroying another?

Man should be as eager to enrich his soul as he is zealous about building up material fortunes to provide ease and comfort for his body. Worldly goods are only of relative importance. To sustain our daily needs they are significant of course, but to clutter our mind, they are a danger. In the last count of values, only inner riches will matter, all other values will disappear.

In a little while, our own life in its total poverty will be exposed to God's own view. What was hidden, never seen or heard of, will be scrutinized by heaven.

At that moment, the greatest moment of our existence, we will be thankful to God if he covers our shame and our unworthiness with the mantle of his heavenly mercy. "God, be merciful to me, a sinner" (Lk 18:14).

I was sick and you visited me. Sickness is man's hated friend—friend because it has so many lessons to teach; hated because only perfect health meets our expectations. Can any of us enjoy being cut down by a tormenting illness?

Christ knew sickness. Not only did he live with physical pain and mental anguish, but he was familiar with the effects of suffering on mind and body. Whenever he met the crippled, the lame and the abandoned, he became one with their afflictions. Out of a living compassion, not from platonic love, he shared their miseries and healed their wounds. "For it is not as if we had a high priest who was incapable of feeling our weaknesses with us; but we have one who has been tempted in every way that we are, though he is without sin" (Heb 4:15).

The child of God, disfigured in body or mind, might be a pathetic sight on earth but he surely gains a special welcome upon entry into the better world. The helplessness of the creature appeals to the Creator, begging him to make up with love what is lacking in the ailing body.

More than medicine, which is amply provided by our hospitals and skilled doctors, chronically ill patients need hope to keep alive the indomitable will to live. The vital forces which hope stimulates in their souls and bodies perform greater miracles of healing than any available medicine. To bring such hope to the suffering and dying is our responsibility, to deny it is our failure. What kind of hope we lay before our suffering brethren will be known only to ourselves.

I was in prison, and you came to see me. In the cells of our prisons, pain is as rampant as in the corridors of our hospitals. No one would insist that a jail is the loftiest of places in which to live, yet it still claims a high frequency of tenants. Many are sent there not by choice but for want of a better solution. Putting the lawless behind bars calls for fewer sacrifices than trying to better a civilization that has become a breeding ground for dishonesty. Isn't it easier to lock up a person than to reform our style of life? To build more jails also creates greater profits, and for quite a few—this incentive is the one that really counts!

Christ was a prisoner. Laws made by man infringed on the rights given to man by God. Caesar was Caesar and deserved his due, but God was God without rival to his power. Each authority, terrestrial or divine, has its special niche in history and exerts an influence so diverse that one can never be a substitute for the other. To subordinate the voice of God to the ever-shifting needs of the community is as foolish as to expect God's voice to become the only law of the land. If man-made laws are to be the only guide for justice, we who proclaim the rights of the divine are easily declared a menace. No wonder that Christ was brought to trial and condemned to death; it was the only way to silence a voice which could not be threatened into control.

Are any of us really free of guilt? Hasn't the disgrace of condemnation often missed us for one reason only, because we were not caught? Haven't we been lucky enough to cover up many of our indiscretions which we knew to be less than honest? Many times, hidden feelings of jealousy or revenge contaminated our motives, yet our actions were considered worthy of praise. Even though we may not have destroyed life, haven't we at some time destroyed a reputation? Perhaps we have never stolen gold or silver, but what about affections? Hasn't there been, at least once, a moment when we would have been spoken of as guilty except for our cleverness in hiding our real intentions? "If you never overlooked our sins, Yahweh, Lord, could anyone survive? But you do forgive us; and for that we revere you" (Ps 130:3–4).

To judge evil as evil and not overlook the good is a sign of the integrity expected of those who are appointed to rule our land. To sit in judgment over others and count only their misdeeds is forgetting that even in the most hardened criminal, there is a dormant goodness yearning for release.

To judge evil as evil and recognize its roots in ourselves is a sign of the honesty expected of us all, who are, after all, only human.

chapter 11

DEATH . . . . .

the harvest

Stranger, pause as you pass by
Rejoice in life, as once did I;
My harvest came and I am free,
As I am now, so shall you be.

When all the votes are counted and the end result is in, death is forever the undisputed winner. How many battles has death lost? One is free to vote No against God, and quite a few are making such a choice in our time; but to vote No against death is futility itself. This stark reality is so final we have only one choice left to us: *how* to die. Death itself was never placed under man's dominion, nor does it ever ask permission to arrive.

Though we readily admit that most things in our experience yield to mathematical or scientific solutions, we must sadly confess that death is the supreme exception. Our illustrious scientists and daring explorers are as helpless as children when confronted with this inevitability. Not even the satisfaction of feeling right or wrong about its coming is extended to us, since it completely disregards the feelings of its

137

victims. The power of the mind, the greatest force we have to fight death, is rendered ineffective by death's scornful disregard of our intellectual conclusions. Unmoved by applause or disdain, it plays out its own drama. "Every living thing grows old like a garment, the age-old law is 'Death must be'. Like foliage growing on a bushy tree, some leaves falling, others growing, so are the generations of flesh and blood: one dies, another is born. Every achievement rots away and perishes, and with it goes its author" (Si 14:18–20).

In Christianity, death is a unique performance. We die only once and after death comes the event we like the least—judgment.

In facing life's ordeals, we are consoled and encouraged by the assurance that no disaster is beyond redemption. Our faltering energies are revitalized and our emotions cheered if we are told that we have another chance. Not only are sins forgiven but mistakes and errors are corrected in such a way that the renewed performance is often better than the first. As long as our mistakes are not final, we mind them little, and might even learn from them the best of our lessons. But when it comes to stingy death, no second chance is given; one curtain call is all that is accorded us.

As the tree falls, so will it lie forever. Unlike Buddhism or Hinduism, Christianity entertains no belief in reincarnation. For us, dying is a final and unrepeatable act.

Since death is for us an event of such far-reaching consequences, we are often warned of the necessity to be on guard, to watch out, to prepare ourselves and stay awake; to be ready. As if these admonitions were not enough, Christ compares the arrival of death to the coming of a thief in the night at an hour no one expects. Isn't it then wise to adjust to something we cannot avoid? "So stay awake, because you do not know the day when your master is coming" (Mt 24:42).

None of us likes to stare into the abyss that yawns at our feet, nor do we enjoy listening to reminders of our own demise. With a sense of embarrassment, we endure the warnings that soon it will be our turn. At the funerals of our cherished friends we linger, sad and lonely at their graveside, murmuring against God's allowing such a premature or cruel death. No wonder that death has never achieved high rating! Let death remain a truth locked up, opened only on rare occasion and hidden again for the remainder of the year. Why spoil the joyous song of life with the somber melody of death? There is enough gloom in our world. Since death will find us anyway, why seek him out? Let us instead concentrate on a road in life which will make of death a glorious fulfillment.

To refrain from speaking of death to the living might have a point in its favor, but not to mention death to the dying is surely a failure of love. Of course, a message that dispels one's fears will bring exuberant joy to a suffering patient. We all feel relief when good news reaches our sickbed, and we love the person who tells us that we will be fine. But to stir up false hopes when truth alone can give the final hope is irresponsible and dangerous. Regardless of good intention, it is a lie to assure the deeply wounded person that he is doing fine, when his condition is deteriorating alarmingly. To mislead others in their search for peace is always wrong but much more so when everything is at stake. A false security can lead to neglect of what now becomes most urgent. If we feel it is right and just for a person to be punished for destroying another's earthly life, why do we consider it honorable to let someone jeopardize another's eternal life?

More often than we think, a dying patient realizes his predicament and is waiting for us to break the unavoidable news with comforting and loving words. Can we ever be sure that not to know the final verdict is more conducive to inner peace than to know it and accept it? Our surest pronouncements are often only guesses; rarely are we infallible. And patients, often expert in reading facial and bodily expressions, can easily distinguish between what is hidden and what is honest. They probably know much better than we that if wounds refuse to heal and pain persists, the final wound is perhaps already opened. If relatives come more often, perhaps looking for a will, and the doctor drops in more frequently, the patient probably realizes that the end of his journey must be in sight! All in all, it may be harder to fool the dying than the living. Far better to help the patient to remember the eternal promise! Prayer, after all, could be the best medicine.

A doctor who is fully alive to the spiritual realities of his patients shows more concern for their physical well-being when he is honest. In most cases he strengthens the patient's health if he gently refers to an immediate danger. The real doctor of the body will invite rather than obstruct the arrival of the doctor of the soul. Not alone, but together, doctor and priest fulfill a function that Christ exemplified. "Because our present perishable nature must put on imperishability and this mortal nature must put on immortality" (I Co 15:53).

We die alone in different and unexpected ways. The ones who are caught in their early years are mourned by those who cannot understand why life must finish in its morning hours. Those who die in ripe old age are praised by the young for all the happiness they gave in their long span of life. Some leave quickly and without fanfare while others die in agonizing steps which are slow to become final. A few die disappointed, grumbling that neither life nor death was ever welcomed. And there are always those who seem to have a flair for death, dying boldly and assenting to it in a way that leaves a message to be remembered. Others simply close their eyes in peace.

As various as our ways may be, the final fact is the same. "I know it is to death that you are taking me, the common meeting place of all that lives" (Jb 30:23).

The spiritual aspect of death, previously the guarded province of theologians, is now arousing the interest of our scientists. The Easter message, once greeted with benign suspicion is suddenly provoking their curiosity. In growing numbers of seminars and conferences across our blessed land, death and the question of life after death is being discussed with the same serious intent as other scientific matters. Whereas living and dying were formerly considered in terms of hostile combat, they are now being tentatively considered as a unity. Not that atheists will ever abandon their denial of man's spiritual entity—they are far too insecure in their negations to take the risk of submitting their minds to doubts—but the many agnostics of our era, may now probe more deeply before they speak.

Most of the exploration into the mysterious world of death involves interviews with people who have experienced a clinically defined death but were resuscitated and later reported what they had seen and heard. These death experiences, gathered from hundreds of people, have three elements in common which substantiate the message of Holy Scripture: a sense of the soul or "self" floating out of the body, a tremendous inner peace which no other power could disturb, and a meeting with people in the other world whom they had known in this world. Added to this data is the fact that those who had been brought back from death were not afraid of dying anymore. Perhaps they found in death what Scripture tells us death must be: a friend.

The out-of-body experiences which these people have recounted, including watching their body being resuscitated, were not unfamiliar to St. Paul. He tells of a case known to him: "I know a man in Christ who, fourteen years ago, was caught up—whether still in the body or out of the body, I do not know; God knows—right into the third heaven. I do know, however, that this same person—whether in the body or out of the body, I do not know; God knows—was caught up into paradise and heard things which must not and cannot be put into human language" (II Co 12:2–4).

Our Church is accepting, not triumphantly but with cautious optimism and genuine appreciation, all these interesting observations.

The efforts to save a life than can be saved deserve our deepest admiration, but to prolong, at considerable expense of money and suffering, a life already doomed deserves serious rethinking. In our country, with all of its advance technology, dying has grown steadily more fearsome, more lonely, more impersonal.

Where are the days when a person was allowed to die in peace and dignity at home, surrounded by a loving family and consoled by the prayers of faithful friends? Today the dying patient is whisked away to a hospital where he finds strange surroundings, is met by people he has never seen and given tests and treatments which alleviate some discomforts while creating others. In subdued voices the doctors and nurses discuss medical procedures that might postpone the inevitable event without ever trying to find out what the dying patient wants. Pacemakers, respirators, tubes, and all the other products of medical technology are surely blessed instruments to heal the living, but should they be routinely applied to delay the grace of dying?

Accepting the inevitable and simply easing the passage from life to life is preferable to the use of futile extraordinary means to continue a finished life on earth. This demand for dignity in death is far from usurping God's power over life and decreeing the death of a human creature as in so-called mercy killings. If death cannot be mastered, then death should be left alone. Only if a person is assured that the final struggle is between death and himself will he enter this struggle with confidence and faith.

We so commonly identify death with taking something from us that we tend to forget that it can also bring us a gift. Losing a loved one often means finding something in ourselves that we never suspected was there. Grief is surely deeply experienced when we realize that someone we have loved has gone from us, but at the same time this suffering from bereavement also cures. Once we accept our loss without bitterness we begin to recognize, perhaps ever so slowly, that the departure of the beloved has opened new avenues for the energies and concerns which were earlier concentrated on the beloved. Those who were never fully enough alive to see their own potential will feel lost when death takes away the one for whom they faithfully but passively existed. Patience brings this to understanding.

After the sharpness of grief has passed, the bereaved will sense a stirring of new interest and freedom which had been submerged by the gentle demands of love and a fully shared life. In the midst of winter there comes an assurance of the eternal spring in our hearts. Our confidence in the one who has died is transferred into a stronger confidence in ourselves who must go on living, and in the God who has given us life and will see us through. Death is after all a marvelous teacher for the living. "The virtuous man who dies condemns the godless who survive, and youth's untimely end the protracted age of the wicked. These people see the wise man's ending without understanding what the Lord has in store for him or why he has taken him to safety" (Ws 4:16–18).

As long as our approach to death remains on a purely academic level we can hardly experience a dread of it. To write a treatise about dying can be just a piece of work if the author remains aloof from the realities of his writings. A speaker may be eloquent on the subject and generate a response that sublimates the fears of his listeners, yet he may still ignore the lesson himself. Thinking about death without being personally involved frees one from the very perils one dramatizes so cleverly for others.

As a lesson taught, the subject of death remains an

object "out there"; as a lesson lived, it can become an awesome inner experience. When we ourselves are called to be the victims, death assumes a different aspect. What was calmly observed before and perhaps even accepted as a distant threat is now suddenly upon us demanding response.

Some of us are born bargain hunters. Clinging to life, we are apt to use some of these tactics when death nears our door. "Wait a little longer, death, give me more time," we say. "I am not ready yet; my accounts are still confused and certain things of my past are yet to be smoothed out. Why can't you add another year to my life? No one will be hurt if you grant me a longer breathing spell!"

It takes time and thought to realize that the hand of death is stronger than we are, and for the first time, perhaps, we see things in the light of eternity without the illusions of the present moment. We become more concerned about our reception in the other world. Only complete understanding will let us see ourselves as beggars before God with the hope that his mercy will somehow dilute his divine justice.

Is there any straw left for us to grasp? Can we do anything to make our final encounter with death a profitable bargain, something so good that even God cannot refuse it? "Yes, if you forgive others their failings, your heavenly Father will forgive you yours; but if you do not forgive others, your Father will not forgive your failings either" (Mt 6:14–15).

And so, after all, there is a bargain left for us, a bargain between us and those who have wronged us or inflicted upon us some pain that still hurts. We could have tried for revenge, we could have demanded an eye for an eye, a tooth for a tooth—unless we remembered the divine request to forgive others who may "not know what they are doing." If we are generous in forgiveness, God will be generous in forgiving us; only this heavenly assurance can make of death an easier burden to bear. If we refuse pardon to those who have troubled us, what chance is left?

Not always by virtue do we finally surrender to God what was his from the beginning; it is more often by necessity. There is an eternal seed in us that no power in this world can ever reduce to pure matter. What is material in us will be handed over by death to the recycling of nature. At the same time what is spiritual in us will be reborn into everlasting life. The soul, which becomes the melody without an instrument, rises to the higher life for which it was made and for which it had to leave the body. "Don't delude yourself into thinking God can be cheated; where a man sows, there he reaps; if he sows in the field of self-indulgence he will get a harvest of corruption out of it; if he sows in the field of the Spirit he will get from it a harvest of eternal life" (Ga 6:7–8).

Only at the moment of death can we truly say *I am*. For us, life has always been a "becoming." Before death we live in anticipation of what will happen in the future; today looks forward to tomorrow. Life with all of its wonders beckons us to follow and snatch its surprises. In death, the challenge of life is not ended but is raised to a higher dimension unaffected by limitations of space and time. The new creation begins its reign in which the new man enters the new dwelling for the endless day.

In our final act of dying, we reach the moment when

nothing can be added and nothing can be taken away; what we are we shall remain forever. The veil drops from our eyes and the meaning of life opens with a clarity never before experienced. We see what life has made of us and what we have made of life. What we have done and what we have failed to do are focused in a single image and speak to us as friends or enemies. Not whom I loved but how I loved will matter; not what I gave but why I gave will be counted. "That is why there is no weakening on our part, and instead, though this outer man of ours may be falling into decay, the inner man is renewed day by day. Yes, the troubles which are soon over, though they weigh little, train us for the carrying of a weight of eternal glory which is out of all proportion to them" (II Co 4:16–17).

Many things in life give us pleasure for the moment and anticipation of the future, but death is not one of them. Even the best of us should refrain from undue optimism. With so much at stake and so little to offer, apprehension is preferable to presumption. To worry a little before we arrive seems better than not to worry and fail to arrive. That millions have died before us and managed quite well is of little consolation at the moment when only our own performance is felt. No one can assure us now where our lasting home will be; we all must wait until Christ himself will pierce the mystery and either welcome us to his kingdom or turn us away.

There was once a time in history that death found its master. In a tense duel fought on a hill called Calvary, death was strong enough to defeat the Nazarene carpenter but too weak to prevail against Christ the redeemer. Christ possessed the unique power to restore himself from death to life, not by means of reincarnation but by the heralded way of resurrection. His broken body returned in a glorified state. His earthly life had been the prelude to the glorious one. Now heaven and earth were finally one. In the risen Lord, past, present, and future merged in an eternal *now*.

Full humanity keeps its options open to the past and future while never losing consciousness of the now. What the past has taught us and what the future expects of us creates the responsible present. Inherent in all our deeds is not only their earthly significance but also their eternal expectancies. Both worlds must assert their voice in our decisions.

If we accept life's challenge as a gift from earth and heaven, we will not fear death. Rather, we will know it as the friend who opens for us a vision such as eye has never seen and ear has never heard. Life finally will be ours, since we know how to die.

chapter 12

HUMANITY IN CRISIS . . . . .

the storm

With faith I face the storm of life
A mystery of living;
With God I strive beyond myself–
The secret is in giving.

Redemption, which opened up to us the mysteries
of heaven, did not shut out the miseries which humanity faces on earth. Security in social or economic terms
was not included in the strategy of divine salvation,
nor was an easy life ever promised by Christ to his
followers. Redemption opened the door to the decisive
point of human experience where the finite ends and
the infinite has its beginning, but all that is tragic and
desperate in the human situation persists in its inevitable darkness despite the death of Christ on the cross.

To say that mankind is in a precarious state is ex-
pressing something that most of us feel but few are
willing to acknowledge. Many of our philosophers,
though their approaches vary, share a common pessimism. "Man's fate," says one, "is a failure, a check
and defeat. He is striving against insuperable odds
and cannot avoid being completely checked." Another

149

calls life a "plunge into darkness," where courage is demanded more than truth, and the hero is "the man who fails bravely and genuinely." A third sees life as a sport where "the hunter pursues his prey," with the animal faith that the life of man and of beast is basically the same. For survival one needs only to be stronger, not wiser or more humane.

Such abysmal lack of faith may appall us and such a depth of pessimism disturb us, but we can hardly deny that humanity today faces a crisis which projects a frightening dimension on the face of tomorrow. We hear a babel of voices that promise a better life when everything will be fine, everyone will be richer; yet as soon as the sound of their voices fade, we are left alone with the same hunger they promised to still. We are told that a great and daring society will be built in which all our ills will be healed; but when the speeches are over, we realize that the fabric of our society is torn apart by crime and violence.

Political alignments, with ever-changing balances of power, replay old melodies of peace only to unleash ugly threats of war at the most propitious moments. Enemies of yesterday become friends of today and alliances built for a distant future hardly survive the pressures of the moment.

Many in our generation believe that it is too late for modern man to be saved, too late to turn on the lights at the end of the tunnel. A few declare that we have strayed too far from home to find the way back, and besides, the right way is lost anyhow, so what difference does it make?

Hidden among all those prophets of gloom are the messengers of disaster who intimate, secretly or openly, that the explosion of the bomb is the perfect solution to the hostilities in this nuclear age. "I look out of myself," wrote Cardinal Newman, "and there I see a sight which fills me with unspeakable distress. The world seems simply to give the lie to that great truth that there is a God of whom my whole being is so full. The effect upon me is as confusing as if this world denied that I am in existence myself. If I looked into a mirror and did not see my face, I should have the sort of feeling which comes upon me when I look into this living busy world and see no reflection of its creator."*

Under these circumstances is change only a remote possibility or is it nearer than we think? Opposite dimensions of the human mind attract each other. The most desperate are forever ready to become the most hopeful; the worst sinners yearn most anxiously for a redeemer.

But such a hoped-for change will never happen by accident. It must be initiated by the Christ of the twentieth century, the men and women who are willing to share with this tormented generation its miseries and its hunger. The Good Samaritan who played such an illustrious part in our Gospel must return again to our streets and assure the victims of injustice that they are not alone any more, that someone is with them to share their pain, someone is out there who makes their cause his own. "But a Samaritan traveller who came upon him was moved with compassion when he saw him. He went up and bandaged his wounds, pouring oil and wine on them. He then lifted him on to his own

---

* *Apologia pro Vita Sua* (London: Longmans, Green, Reader, and Dyer, 1880), p. 241.

mount, carried him to the inn and looked after him" (Lk 10:33–34).

We have reached the point in time where words no longer provide solutions. People are looking for bread, not promises. Their hunger is not fed by the debates of sophisticated theologians or stilled by the theories of self-assured philosophers. Wounds have eaten so deeply into their flesh that arguments alone will not prevail. Only deeds will do, deeds of love and understanding that can restore confidence and hope. The God conceived in the mind must become the God of the heart.

Actions must replace abstractions. That God reigns in the kingdom of heaven is easy to accept, but whether God is alive here on earth is a question some find hard to answer. The imperative today is not "prove it to me" but "show it to me."

A faith fully alive and translated into deeds is the only faith our era will accept. A faith genuinely concerned with man's temporal and spiritual hunger is the only faith our modern generation submits to with trust. This, perhaps, could be a most effective antidote to the venom of a blatant paganism.

The religious mind, steeped in erudite notions and well-conceived definitions, often sees the world of the divine only in dogmatic dimensions of proof and counterproof. In an impressive array of formulations and solutions, forceful at times to the point of brilliance, the theologian searches for ways to show that God exists. In the course of his explorations, however, during his hallowed crusade for possession of the "Holy Land," he exposes his very soul to the danger of losing what he is so eager to prove, the mystery of the divine. The God his mind perceives, the God his soul finds, easily turns into an intellectual abstraction, reigning with full authority in the heavens but having little or no connection with the burning problems of earth.

Saint Paul, writing to the materially prosperous and morally corrupt Corinthians, sensed this danger in his own apostolic work when he said, "Lest perhaps after preaching to others, I myself should be rejected." The divine spark burning in the hearts of all of us must never be smothered by the weight of arguments and disputations which few can understand and fewer still are ready to accept.

The man in crisis, often described by our philosophers and poets as empty, hollow, and stuffed, can also be characterized as one in frantic search for something better, purer, and holier than he himself can ever be—for God. The *homo viator*, the pilgrim on earth who by now is dimly aware that he has lost his way, looks desperately toward the skies, hoping to find the star that can lead him back again to the birthplace of a newborn redeemer.

Solzhenitsyn wrote, in a beautiful prayer, "You, O Lord, bestow on me the certitude that you exist and are mindful of me, that all the paths of righteousness are not barred. As I ascend onto the hill of earthly glory, I turn back and gaze astounded on the road that led me here beyond despair, where I too may reflect your radiance upon mankind. All that I may yet reflect, you shall accord me and appoint others where I shall fail."*

* Alexander Solzhenitsyn's Lenten Letter, *Time*, April 3, 1972.

To reflect God's radiance upon mankind, to convince the poor and forgotten that the love of God and the love of man have not withered away in a solemn recital of arid formulas and prayers but are still burning in the hearts of believers—this is the mission the apostle has to fulfill in the last part of our troubled and perplexed century.

Christ was born into our world and lived in our midst for many years. He is now risen; he is not standing in front of us anymore, begging us to defend his life. His existence and his revelations are generally accepted as historical, proven beyond any reasonable doubt. What remains now is for us to apply the happiest event in history to less happy events which make history. The announcement of the Good News to all who hunger and thirst for justice and peace must become so real to the people of our time that Christ becomes an integral part of their life with all of its splendor and shadow.

But who will be the announcer? Who will be the one to carry the glad tidings of love and forgiveness to human hearts which can be so full of hate? "Then I heard the voice of the Lord saying: 'Whom shall I send? Who will be our messenger?' I answered, 'Here I am, send me' "(Is 6:8–9).

Are we ready to answer the call? Are we prepared to cope with the tremendous expectations that a materialistic society thrusts on our shoulders? Will we be free enough to give without counting the price that must be always paid for the gift? If we are to represent the mystery of the divine, our spirituality must be of the kind that can inspire a civilization at a time when even the most brilliant can see no further than the shadows of the night.

One set into the tensions of spiritual life must be alerted to the dangers of circling around in self-admiration. The practice of faith can turn into a multitude of activities and ceremonies that seek more to please ourselves than to follow the demands of the divine. Projecting the image of faith into our self-imposed roles absorbs so much of our attention that the cry of the helpless may never reach our ears. The real Christ portrayed so well in Scripture often remains hidden in the pages, far from those who need him most.

All of us, believers and unbelievers alike, sense today a threat of frightful proportion to the very survival of our culture. As believers, we are challenged by our own times to shape the most radical response provided by the Gospel. We can hardly expect much from the shortsighted creature who believes only in the ground he walks on and trusts only the wall he leans against.

Hope is what we need to take the longest stride history has ever taken, the daring steps through the insecurities that faith and its works demand. "Be either a hero or a saint," Nietzsche recommended, "for in between is only banality."

People today will not settle for banality. They want more because they need more. Can we bring to them the gifts they yearn for, or are we forcing God to appoint others to take over the task which we have failed to carry through?